Colette's France
Her lives, her loves

Colette's France
her lives, her loves

JANE
GILMOUR

hardie grant books
MELBOURNE · LONDON

Colette's France

Published in 2013 by Hardie Grant Books

Hardie Grant Books (Australia)
Ground Floor, Building 1
658 Church Street
Richmond, Victoria 3121
www.hardiegrant.com.au

Hardie Grant Books (UK)
Dudley House, North Suite
34–35 Southampton Street
London WC2E 7HF
www.hardiegrant.co.uk

A Cataloguing-in-Publication entry is available from the catalogue of the National Library of
Australia at www.nla.gov.au
Colette's France: Her lives, her loves
ISBN 978 1 74270 535 4

Publishing Director: Fran Berry
Project Editor: Helen Withycombe
Editor: Janet Austin
Design Manager: Heather Menzies
Cover and internal design: Clare O'Loughlin
Cover image: © Lipnitzki/Roger-Viollet
Back cover images: Centre d'Étude Colette
Typesetter: Helen Beard
Production: Todd Rechner

Colour reproduction by Splitting Image Colour Studio
Printed in China by 1010 Printing International Limited

Contents

Bonjour, ma - Miss chérie et mon petit Léo.
Il fait magnifique depuis notre arrivée mais le trajet, a ressemblé à une expédition polaire. Un froid horrible. Les nuits sont encore très fraîches.

Je ne vous aurai donc jamais dans ce pays ? Malgré la sécheresse il est charmant, et notre jardin tout glycines, roses rouges et blanches, et les pitto-sporums chargent l'air d'un parfum que tu ne connais peut-être pas ? Je vous embrasse tendrement, mes enfants. Maurice aussi

Colette

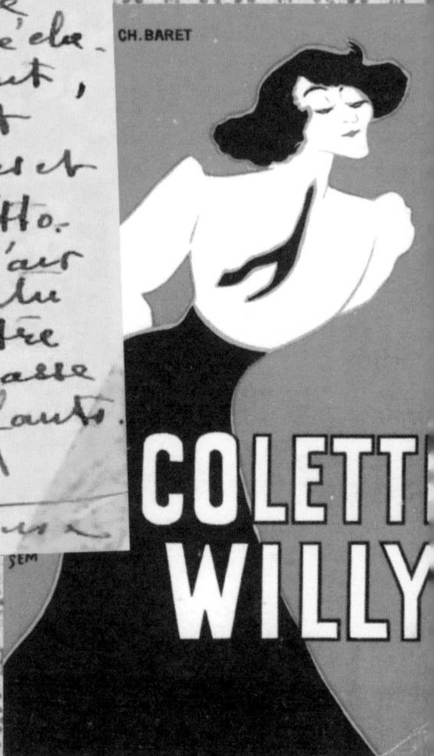

12. - SAINT TROPEZ
Rue de la Miséricorde
Pittoresque arceau

CH. BARET

COLETTE
WILLY

SEM

Prologue

In the footsteps of Colette

My first encounter with the world of Colette and her writing was when I was still at school. I was studying French, and extracts from her work were occasionally chosen as texts for dictation. I remember particularly an extract from *Claudine à l'école* (*Claudine at School*) about the woods that surrounded the little village of Montigny. When I reread that passage even now, so many years later, I am transported back to my schoolroom, just as Colette was transported back to the schooldays of her youth through the story of Claudine.

Colette's imagery and the rhythm of her prose entranced me even then, as I struggled with the complex structure of her sentences and the challenges of her vocabulary. Her words conjured up sounds and smells, colours and tastes. The France she described held out the promise for me, in faraway Australia, of a landscape that changed with the seasons, of a way of life deeply rooted in tradition, a culture that was embedded in the land. It seemed to me that Colette embodied a certain idea of France—an idea that was romantic, perhaps, but one that I wanted to know better.

As I read more of Colette's work—*The Ripening Seed, Chéri, The Cat*—I willingly entered into the obsessive and closed emotional worlds she created, where her characters were captive to an ideal of love. Colette has been accused of writing only about love. For me, her books were not so much about love as about its impossibility, about the irredeemable distance between the idea of love and its reality. More powerfully, they spoke to me of the struggle to be a woman, of what one critic had called 'the loneliness of a woman face to face with her destiny'. It seemed to me that behind all of Colette's work stood the image of a woman who refused to forgo her own freedom. Her work spoke of a life fully lived, of a sensual curiosity and energy, and a profound feminine sensibility. When reading Colette, I had the feeling of not being alone. She was like a confidante, a friend who could see into the human heart, who could peel back the layers of illusion and delusion that mask the complex and troublesome nature of human relationships.

After leaving school, I continued my French studies at university, where my reading of French literature ranged from the troubadour poets of the fifteenth and sixteenth centuries to the great works of the nineteenth and twentieth—Balzac and Proust, Gide and Sartre. But I was constantly drawn back to Colette. Then, with my undergraduate years behind me, and the financial support of a scholarship, I decided to head straight to Paris, where I enrolled at the Sorbonne as a doctoral student. I wasn't sure what the focus

of my study would be, but I knew it would have something to do with Colette.

So there I was, a 22-year-old stepping out of the train at the Gare du Nord and into the city of my dreams. I can still clearly remember the taxi ride from the train station on my first day in Paris—past Notre Dame, across the Seine to the Latin Quarter, up the boulevard Saint-Michel. As we drove past Notre Dame, I was disappointed to see that most of the façade was covered in scaffolding and sheeting. The cathedral was being steam-cleaned—a process that was slowly transforming all of the city, cleaning off the centuries-old layers of soot and dirt to reveal the honey-coloured stone beneath. More distressing was the fact that I could hardly understand a word of what the taxi driver was saying to me. How could this be, after all the years I had spent learning French? It would take a couple of weeks before I became accustomed to the accent and language of working-class Parisians, the people I interacted with on the street, in the shops and cafes, on the *métro*.

Life as a student in Paris was full of surprises—the lack of structure, the process of finding a supervisor for my thesis, the challenge of obtaining a residency card (did I *really* need to have a document that gave my mother's maiden name?), the ritual of organising a reader's card for the Bibliothèque nationale de France.

It was late 1968, and in Paris political dissent and 'structuralism' were changing the intellectual landscape. The student riots of May '68 were only a few months back, and the Sorbonne was still in a somewhat chaotic state. Tensions between the forces of order and the student population remained very evident in the Latin Quarter. Grey windowless buses in which the armed security forces whiled away the hours and days were a threatening presence on the streets. Skirmishes between these forces and protesting student groups broke out from time to time. One afternoon I beat a hasty retreat into a cafe when I saw a group of students running down the street being pursued by a squad of truncheon-wielding security forces men. Even eighteen months later, a happy fourteenth of July celebration could turn into a nasty confrontation between members of the special security forces and innocent revellers.

The Latin Quarter and Saint-Germain were still at the centre of Paris's vibrant literary and artistic life, with Jean-Paul Sartre and Simone de Beauvoir actively involved in the ongoing political situation. However, my world of study revolved around the work of a woman who was aligned with neither the existentialists nor the structuralists, and had not yet been claimed by the feminists. Her work, nonetheless, was held high in the pantheon of French writers.

I had decided that the focus of my work would be on Colette's literary style, in particular the way she used imagery. I was interested in the power of metaphor and symbol in literature, and was fascinated by her use of colour and the way she used images to create a concrete representation of an idea, feeling or state of mind. For me, Colette succeeded in making the abstract become real, using the physical world of the senses to reveal the inner world of the mind. 'Between the real and the imagined,' she wrote, 'there is always the place taken by the word, magnificent and larger than the object.'

During my first year in Paris I lived in student digs at the Cité Universitaire, near Parc Montsouris in the south of the city. In the afternoons, after studying at the Bibliothèque nationale, I would walk from the library along the river and up the boulevard Saint-Michel to take the train home from Luxembourg station. The walk across the Pont des Arts, as the setting sun lit up the domed silhouette of the Institut de France, made my heart glow with the joy of being in Paris.

Then my student life changed. I married an Australian lawyer. We had met at university and had travelled to Europe together—he to London to do a master's degree in international law and me to Paris. We were young and in love, and Paris was such a romantic city. When a position came up for an international lawyer in Paris, it was almost like it was meant to be. We were married, and moved into a tiny apartment just off avenue Mozart in the 16th arrondissement. Living as a student, eating in student restaurants in the Latin Quarter and hanging out with other students, had been great fun, but now my Parisian life was different—rather than strolling across the Pont des Arts, I was going to the markets on my way home from the library, learning to cook in the French style, hosting dinner parties, going to exhibitions and concerts, being part of a different rhythm of Parisian life.

I still spent most days at the Bibliothèque nationale, in the beautiful old reading room with its domed ceiling. It was just a couple of minutes' walk from the Palais-Royal, where Colette had lived for the last twenty years of her life. The gardens of the Palais-Royal were a quiet and peaceful place to sit in the sunshine when I needed a break from the books. I would often look

up at what had been Colette's apartment and imagine her leaning out the window, looking out on this garden that she had claimed as her own. I would have loved to have visited what had been her home. I understood that it belonged to her daughter, but my attempts to make contact with her were unsuccessful. It was not until many years later that I learnt the sorry reality of Colette's will, in which she had disinherited her daughter in favour of Maurice Goudeket, her third and last husband.

Goudeket did agree to meet me. He had married again, and had a son, and had become the keeper of Colette's legend. We met in his elegant apartment on the avenue Kléber, and sat in his study, which was lined with books by Colette and with photos and portraits of her, but I learnt little from this precise and careful man. I left with the feeling that he had been merely humouring me, a young foreigner, by agreeing to see me. So, rather than trying to piece together the complex and fascinating story of Colette's life, I went back to focusing my attention on her writing. And yet, inevitably, I came to know the woman through her work.

Three years later, after I had finished my thesis and defended it in front of four learned professors in an imposing room in the Sorbonne, with busts of the great men of letters looking down on me, my husband and I left Paris. Arriving back in Australia was a rude awakening. Academic positions were hard to get, French language and literature studies not being particularly fashionable at a time when France was undertaking nuclear tests in the Pacific, so I pursued a different career path—working in the arts, and then for an international scientific and environmental research organisation.

It was a fascinating and fulfilling career that I have never regretted, but, sadly, my marriage was a casualty in those early years of adjusting to being back in Australia. My three and a half years in Paris, Colette and my French studies, together with my marriage, became a part of my past. It was as though I had closed that file and locked it away.

As the years passed and other demands on my time receded, the germ of this book started to take shape. In many ways, my life seemed to be circling back to the years I had spent in Paris. My former husband was not well and we would talk on the phone about Paris, the people we had known, the adventures we had shared. I pulled the copy of my thesis out of storage and started to re-read it. Colette and her imaginary universe were there in front of me again. A sensual and physical world, but also a world in which a woman was constantly struggling to find and retain her independence.

Gradually, I began to explore the idea of writing a book about my journey in the footsteps of Colette. In 2007, my partner and I went to stay in a little village in Burgundy, not far from Saint-Sauveur-en-Puisaye, where Colette had been born and had spent her childhood. A great deal had been published about Colette since I'd written my thesis, and there had been a renewal of interest in her work, in France as well as elsewhere in the world. I visited the museum dedicated to her life and work that had opened in Saint-Sauveur, and became a member of the Society of Friends of Colette. Subsequent trips to France took on a new purpose as I visited the places that had been part of Colette's life—Saint-Tropez, Brittany, Castel-Novel, Les Monts-Bouccons near Besançon. My partner was happy to share this voyage of discovery with me—he was becoming quite a Francophile himself.

I began to see Colette's life emerging through the prism of the different places in which she had lived—the places of her heart—each representing a particular period in her life and particular relationships, each profoundly influencing her writing, and each so vividly evoked in the shapes, colours, perfumes and sounds of her prose.

Colette and France, France and Colette. She claimed to know only small parts of France:

> A bit of Burgundy, a few corners of Paris, two or three cantons in the Jura and
> Franche-Comté, stretches of flaxen coast in Picardy and Brittany, the green meadows
> of Brive, the glowing red heath of the Corrèze high plateau, and lastly, Provence,
> a little bit of Provence, so sweet that I have no desire to go any further afield.

It turned out to be quite a lot of France!

Colette has always seemed to me to be quintessentially French. Perhaps it is because of what she called her provinciality—her respect for all that is fine in life. Her tastes were simple—good food, an honest wine, friends, flowers and 'the sound of water bubbling up from a spring or fountain'. She often talked of her poetry as being 'earthbound'. She loved to garden, to get her hands dirty, to smell the earth, to enjoy the fruits of her own labour.

But Colette was a much more complex person than she would at times have us believe. Armed with what she called her 'monstrous innocence', she wore many masks as she created both her own reality and her own myth—provincial ingénue, risqué performer, lesbian lover, prodigious journalist and writer, businesswoman, baroness and mother, lover and seducer, loyal friend and mentor and, finally, grand old lady of letters, revered and honoured with a state funeral when she died in 1954.

I invite you to take a journey with me in search of Colette—to visit Saint-Sauveur-en-Puisaye and to conjure up, behind the solid walls, the garden that was her childhood paradise; to stand on the beach at Rozven in Brittany, and see in the pale blue and golden light the beginnings of a relationship between an older woman and a younger man; to linger in the Palais-Royal in Paris and imagine Colette looking out onto a deserted and defeated wartime Paris, seeing women poorly clad against the cold, hurrying through the dawn light to the jobs left vacant by the men who had been captured or sent to work camps.

As we follow Colette through her beloved France, we need, however, to be mindful of her own warning: *Do not think, as you read this, that I am painting my own portrait. Be patient, it is only my model.*

Writing about Colette means unravelling the reality from the myth, but it also means allowing the myth to exist. The myth was the creation of Colette's own genius; it was the product of her style, of her love of language and her love of life. She was a woman who grasped hold of life with both hands, who was free thinking and independent, and never untrue to herself. She was unflinchingly female—tough, egotistical and seductive.

Through the places of her heart, we will come to know her.

A woman claims as many native lands as she has had happy love affairs. Likewise, she is born under every sky where she recovers from the pain of loving.

CARTE POSTALE

UTILISEZ LA P...
AERIEN...
SE RENSEIGNER DANS
LES BUREAUX DE POSTE

RÉPUBLIQUE FRANÇAISE
POSTES
PASTEUR
15

Les Marchais
9 Boulevard
Labric Maubourg
Paris

75. St-SAUVEUR-e...
Entrée du Châ...

TICKET D'
n° 0.8
EXPOSITION UNIV

Chapter 1
— Childhood in Saint-Sauveur-en-Puisage —

I have just passed through, without pausing, a countryside which belongs to me, the countryside of my childhood. It seemed as though my heart was embraced by a long caress.

As we approached the village of Saint-Sauveur, where Sidonie-Gabrielle Colette was born in 1873, the mist was lifting and the sun was beginning to break through on a crisp, clear autumn morning. Saint-Sauveur is about two hours south of Paris, but we had come from a different direction, across the Loire and through the woods that Colette described so lovingly. A sign announced that we were about to enter Colette's country.

It is only in recent years that Saint-Sauveur has reclaimed its most famous inhabitant. On my first visit to Saint-Sauveur in the early 1970s, when I was studying in Paris, there was little to tell the casual visitor that this was the birthplace of Colette. I knew that the house where she was born was still standing and that it would be easy to recognise, because she had described it as a large, imposing and severe building on the rue de l'Hospice, with its lopsided steps leading to the front door, 'six steps on one side, ten on the other'. When I found the house, a rose marble plaque simply announced: 'Here Colette was born'. No mention of a date. How very French, I thought, not to mention Colette's age. After all, when the plaque was unveiled in 1925, Colette was still alive.

The village was not very welcoming on that first visit. There was little sign of life—a few cars in the square in the centre of the village, a *bar-tabac*, a post office, a bakery and a general store, and that was about it. The shutters of the house where Colette grew up were firmly closed—no chance of knocking on the door and being shown the centre of her childhood life, the garden that lay hidden behind the arched carriage entrance. This was definitely a house that, as Colette had written, only 'smiled inwards, towards the garden'.

When Colette lived here as a girl, Saint-Sauveur-en-Puisaye was a flourishing village of close to two thousand people. The Puisaye was in fact a poor region—Colette called it 'my poor Burgundy'. It was certainly not the Burgundy of the great vineyards. This western edge of Burgundy was dependent primarily on agricultural production and on charcoal from the dense woods. However, as road and rail links connected it to the outside world, Saint-Sauveur profited from the progress that was happening elsewhere in France. Towards the end of the nineteenth century, the village boasted fourteen bakers, seventeen stone-masons, thirteen carpenters, seventeen seamstresses. In addition, it had its mix of bourgeois families, a few

The façade of Colette's childhood home, a house which 'only smiled inwards to the garden'

Sido, Colette's mother, when she was thirty years old   *Captain Jules-Joseph Colette*

members of old provincial nobility, farmers and manual labourers.

As I walked along the main street, I saw that the village still had a certain picturesque charm with its narrow, steep streets, the roofs of the houses tumbling down the hillside, as Colette had described them. And towards the top of the hill, a somewhat run-down castle with a crumbling old tower beside it.

I reflected on the curious twists of fate that had brought Colette's parents, Adèle Sidonie Landoy and Jules-Joseph Colette, to this provincial backwater. Adèle—or Sido, as she became known through Colette's writing—was born in Paris in 1835. Her mother had died when she was just two months old and Sido was given by her father into the care of a wet nurse who lived in Mézilles, 10 kilometres away from Saint-Sauveur. When she was about eight years old, Sido joined her father and brothers in Belgium, where they were then living. After the death of her father, she lived with her older brother, Eugène, who was a highly regarded journalist and editor. The young woman grew up in a cultured and free-thinking household that was frequented by artists and writers.

It was during one of her regular visits to her nanny at Mézilles that Sido came to the attention of the family of Jules Robineau-Duclos. Twenty-one years older than Sido, and a rich landowner in the Puisaye region, Robineau-Duclos was a morose and violent man who was prone to alcohol-induced rages. His family hoped that marriage might bring order to his life, but no father in the region would consider marrying his daughter to such a man, in spite of the extent of his landholdings. Sido's brothers in far away Brussels were approached and, ignorant of the man's alcoholic outbursts and believing that they were acting in the best interests of their sister—a rich husband for a young woman without a dowry—they agreed to the marriage proposal.

Sido must have found very little reason for joy when she first arrived in Saint-Sauveur in 1857, trapped as she was between an alcoholic husband and the narrow-minded villagers with whom she had little in common. These were people who had lived all their lives in this provincial backwater, and who for the most part were 'influenced by its meanness and spitefulness'. How lonely she must have been after the stimulating and interesting life she had led in Brussels with her brothers and their literary friends.

There would be two children from the marriage—Juliette, who was born in 1860, and Achille, born in 1863. Village gossip was abuzz after the birth of Achille, as it was rumoured that he had been fathered not by Robineau-Duclos, but by Captain

Sido at forty-five years of age, when Colette, her last child, was seven

Jules-Joseph Colette, who had arrived in Saint-Sauveur in 1860. Like Sido, the Captain was not a local. Born in Toulon in the South of France in 1826, Jules-Joseph was destined for a career in the army, after graduating from the prestigious Saint-Cyr training academy. The handsome, brave young soldier joined the Zouaves, and served in Algeria, Turkey and Africa. He was quickly promoted to the rank of captain, but his military career came to an abrupt end when he was badly wounded in the northern Italian town of Melegnano. His left leg had to be amputated, and he was pensioned out of the army and offered a sinecure as tax collector in Saint-Sauveur.

It did not take long for this cultivated and gallant newcomer to attract the attention and affection of Sido. The truth behind the rumour of Achille's parentage will never be known, but certainly the boy was much closer in looks and temperament to his younger sister and brother than to his older sister, Juliette.

Robineau-Duclos died from a violent apoplectic attack in 1865, and after the appropriate period of mourning, Sido was free to marry Jules-Joseph, defying the gossip and calumny that circulated freely amongst the citizens of Saint-Sauveur. The gossip was such that the local justice of the peace prepared a damning report to the public prosecutor, condemning Sido's morals and accusing her of having allowed Robineau-Duclos to die without making any effort to help him. In passing judgement on Sido, the good citizens of Saint-Sauveur ignored the fact that Robineau-Duclos

PREMIER PORTRAIT DE COLETTE

Que j'avais de charme à six-huit mois!

Colette

had continued to maintain a mistress, his former maid, throughout his marriage, and that from this liaison there was another son. Small wonder that Sido subsequently remained aloof from the other villagers, creating a somewhat closed and separate world for her second husband and children.

From her first husband, Sido had inherited the rights to a significant estate, comprised of a number of farms and woodlands, of which two-thirds were held in trust for the two children of her first marriage. However, there were also significant debts, as well as payments to be made to Robineau-Duclos' mistress and illegitimate son. These ongoing debts would impose a heavy burden on Sido and her new husband, but initially they led a comfortable life, with servants, a carriage, handsome furniture and fine linen, with visits to Paris and to the theatre and shops. Sido did not deprive herself of the little luxuries she enjoyed.

Sido's marriage with Jules-Joseph Colette was a marriage of love. From this union were born two children, Léo, in 1867, and Sidonie-Gabrielle, on 28 January 1873. Gabrielle, our Colette, spent the first eighteen years of her life in Saint-Sauveur. Unlike her elder brothers and sister, she was not sent to boarding school at nearby Auxerre, possibly due to the financial constraints that the family was beginning to experience, or because of Sido's desire to keep this youngest child, her 'golden jewel', close to her.

The photos of the young Colette reveal a poised and beautiful child, her long golden hair flowing down her back or arranged in braids. She looks straight at the camera, without diffidence or false modesty. One can sense an already strong character, intelligent and with the confidence of a young person who was loved and cherished by those who surrounded her.

Colette's was not the typical upbringing of a young girl in a small village. The house was full of books, as both her parents were avid readers. Colette, too, read widely. Her favourite writer was Balzac, but she also read Daudet, Hugo and Mérimée, whose short stories and novellas were popular at the time. Children's stories didn't interest her. She could never find in Perrault's prose 'the velvet darkness, the flash of silver lightning, the ruins, the knights and the delicate-footed horses' of Gustave Doré's illustrations. Books on natural history and accounts of distant explorations fascinated the children, as did the illustrated publications of the great French astronomer of the time, Camille Flammarion. Sido could never understand why her daughter didn't take to Saint-Simon, whose volumes of socialist philosophy were her favourite bedside reading. 'It is curious,' she would say, 'to see how long it takes for children to start reading interesting books!'

Only one writer was banned: Émile Zola. His books were locked away by Captain Colette, who could not see any point in children reading Zola. When Colette, ever curious, asked her mother why she couldn't read Zola's novels, Sido replied, 'There are some that I would prefer you didn't read.' Her daughter's reply was, 'Well, what about the others?' Colette was allowed to read 'the others', but she wasn't satisfied. One day, she took into the garden one of the forbidden books, in which Zola described, with his typical attention to realistic and graphic detail, the birth of a child. The 14-year-old Colette was both shocked and frightened. Was this the fate that awaited her as a young woman? The walls of the garden began to swim in front of her eyes, the sky had become strangely yellow, and she fainted limply onto the grass. It was only her mother's reassurances that convinced Colette that the pain of giving birth was quickly forgotten. 'After all,' Sido said, 'it is never women who write about it, only men, and what do they really know about it?'

This was also a very musical family. The Captain had a fine 'velvety baritone voice' and loved to sing, often teasing visiting neighbours with his romantic airs. All the children played the piano, and Léo was particularly musically gifted; Sido always thought that he should have pursued a musical career. Colette, too, had inherited her father's musical ear. Many years later, she surprised one of her friends with her musical accomplishment when, at a moment's notice, she accompanied a young singer at a private recital. After the young

Achille, always his mother's favourite

girl had stopped singing, Colette continued to play, oblivious to those around her.

From a very young age, the children were taught to think for themselves. Although a doting mother, Sido treated her offspring as adults, and allowed them a great deal of personal freedom. She bantered and jested with them, expecting them to be quick-witted. Both parents were free thinkers. Sido kept up appearances by going to church—even if she had a copy of Corneille's plays concealed between the covers of her prayer book. The children were baptised and the young Gabrielle went to Sunday school and took her first communion. As she later wrote, she had her period of 'being religious', but theirs was not a religious upbringing.

The children were free to spend hours in the garden reading, or to go wandering in the woods. Colette loved to follow along with her two brothers, 'the wild ones' as she called them. Achille was the leader, but Léo was the dreamer, full of fantasies. Occasionally, Sido would wake Colette before dawn so the girl could go off on her own, a basket on each arm, in search of strawberries, gooseberries and blackcurrants. She would come across hidden springs in the woods that 'bubbled out of the ground with a crystalline spurt' or 'rustled through the grass like a snake'. It was on these early-morning walks that Colette first became aware of what she called an

Colette and Léo standing in front of the old iron trellis that sagged under the weight of the wisteria

'inexpressible state of grace', where she felt a deep sense of connection to the world around her. She would come home before the bell rang for first mass, but not before having eaten her fill of berries and tasted the water of the springs.

The secret to the happiness Colette remembered in the house and garden of her childhood was her mother's presence. For the young Gabrielle, it was as if her mother was the centre of the universe, a paradise where the children never fought, where animals and humans communicated gently, a garden where, for thirty years, a husband and his wife lived without ever raising their voices against each other.

But Sido did raise her voice from time to time, to call the children for tea. It was then that she would 'appear, under the old iron arch that tilted to the left under the weight of the wisteria'. She would 'scan the dense greenery, raise her head' and call out, 'The children, where are the children?' Of course, the children would be off reading in some hidden corner of the garden, or playing in the woods.

Sido taught Colette to love the natural world, to respect everything that lived, to be curious, to observe and listen, to feel and taste. 'Can't you hear that it's raining over Moutiers?' she would ask, and Gabrielle would strain her ears to catch the sound of raindrops on the pond in the nearby woods. A few minutes later, she would feel 'the gentle drops of a summer shower on her cheeks and lips'.

It was also from Sido that Colette learnt her passion for gardening. The garden of her childhood basked in a yellow light that shimmered into red and violet. Geraniums and wisteria, roses and hydrangeas coloured her childhood. There was an upper garden and a lower garden. The upper garden was like an extension of the house, which was covered with wisteria and the trumpet-shaped flowers of climbing bignonia. The living room opened out onto a little tiled terrace, with masses of lilac bushes and a little summer house at the end of the garden. Two pine trees and a walnut tree were ideal hiding spots where the children would read. The remains of a doll's teaparty lay scattered on the lawn; a skipping rope hung from the pump; the flowerbeds were inevitably trampled by little feet. But when the sun set and it was time for her friends to go home, the young Colette found herself in a garden that had suddenly become full of danger. Colette lay on the grass, her eyes fixed on the lamp that had just been lit inside. In front of the lamp, a hand 'capped with a bright thimble' passed back and forth. And the young girl, looking in from outside, realised that this hand and this head bent attentively over her sewing were the source of the warmth and light that spread out in diminishing circles to the room, the house, the garden and the village. 'Beyond, all was danger, all was solitude.' For the first time, the young Colette stopped being 'the gay little vampire who, without thinking, sucks dry a mother's heart'.

Stone steps led from the upper to the lower garden. This was the kitchen garden, with its fruit trees—apricots and plums, bitter peaches and cherries—and rows of carrots, lettuces and sorrel, bordered by white lilies and tarragon. Warmed by the sun against the wall, there were eggplants, tomatoes, red peppers and garlic—vegetables of the South to remind Captain Colette of his southern origins. It was here in her mother's garden that Colette learnt to recognise and love the taste of fruit and vegetables freshly picked and still warm from the sun.

The house was full of pets—cats with their numerous kittens, a dog, canaries, a pair of tame swallows that Colette would take to school in her pocket and then set free to fly home. A house without animals was not a home, and Colette would never be without her dogs or cats.

It was a large, comfortable house, with three rooms downstairs and three rooms on the first floor. Colette's room was above the carriage entrance gate. Damask curtains hung in the living room with its elegant furniture, piano, bookcase and porcelain vases. In the dining room, the cherry-wood table seated twelve. Deep cupboards housed the silver monogrammed cutlery, the crystal glasses and fine china plates.

The kitchen was the centre of the house, and it was here that Colette learnt to string up the mushrooms she had collected in the woods for drying, to preserve fruits, to make jams, to make walnut oil. On cold winter afternoons when Colette came home from school, hungry and needing sustenance, Sido would bring up from the cellar a fine bottle from amongst those that had been hidden from the invading Prussian army in 1870—bottles of Château Lafite from Bordeaux, of Chambertin and Corton from Burgundy. In little tastes, Colette learnt to appreciate these great wines, which accompanied her afternoon snack of a little cutlet, a chicken leg or a piece of hard ash-covered cheese, and which left a healthy glow on her cheeks, much to the delight of Sido. Colette's sense of taste was developed from a very early age and was never to leave her.

Like Proust with his madeleine dipped in tea, for Colette there was one taste that always brought back memories of her childhood—the taste of the water chestnuts that were bountiful in the swamps and ponds around Saint-Sauveur. Their odour of reeds, of slow-moving water, of wild mint, their dubious but seductive taste, as she described it, never failed to revive for her the song of the water-chestnut seller in the streets of Saint-Sauveur.

Sido was at the centre not only of her children's physical world, but also of their emotional world. She was convinced of their superiority and she always made them feel special. To her, they were her finest creations and she described them as being 'of the most excellent character'. This sense of specialness, of being different, was no doubt heightened for the young Gabrielle by the fact that she attended the local school in Saint-Sauveur, where rather than mixing with the children of the bourgeois families of the area at boarding school, she found herself in the company of the children of shopkeepers, farmers and labourers. The bright young girl must indeed have stood out amongst her fellow students.

The Captain was a much less substantial figure in Colette's childhood. Years later, she wrote that it seemed strange that she had known her father so little. Her

Family and friends: Colette is seated in front of her father and mother, Juliette is seated on the extreme left, Léo stands behind her and Achille is standing second from the right

attention had been focused on Sido, as indeed had his. Jules-Joseph Colette was a poet, a city dweller, who suddenly found himself thrust from the broad stage of his life in the army, with all his dreams and ambitions, to this little rural backwater. Unlike Sido, who seemed to draw strength from the countryside, Captain Colette felt himself an exile. His need to be surrounded by people, his sociability, as Colette later called it, drew him into village politics, into committee meetings and political campaigning, where 'the hum of human voices resonated'. But he was too much of an outsider to gain the confidence and votes of the local people, and his political ambitions came to nought.

He also aspired to be a writer. On the top shelf of the library was a row of books, inscribed with his handwritten titles. But inside each one there was not a word, apart from a dedication to his wife. Although daunted by the serious tomes he aspired to write, Captain Colette did turn his hand to a sonnet or speech. He would show his daughter his latest composition—a fine piece of oratory or an ode, full of rhythm and rhyme—and his 10-year-old critic would cut straight to the chase. 'Too many adjectives,' she would say. It was certainly her father's sentimentality, she later admitted, that occasionally brought tears to her eyes when she listened to music or watched a dance performance.

One by one, the Captain's ambitions fell by the wayside, but not his pride. Like his daughter, this man who had been destined for a life of military glory never accepted pity. Diminished, he certainly was, but not unhappy. His gallantry and his love for Sido provided reason enough for his happiness. Colette recalled a time when she saw this love in a simple gesture—her father bent over her mother's hand as she picked up the coffee pot from the table, 'with a passionate devotion that knew no age'. Colette never forgot 'this complete image of love: an old man's head, lowered to kiss the small, gracious and wrinkled hand of a housewife'.

Captain Colette

For Colette, the loss of childhood and the loss of her home were linked. Her family's financial difficulties began when she was aged eleven, and her half-sister Juliette married a doctor who lived next door. Thirteen years older than Colette, Juliette had none of the charm and good looks of the three other children, and was always buried deep in her books. The marriage resulted in a complete break between Juliette and her family. Captain Colette's management of the Robineau-Duclos estate had left it even further in debt, and in order to provide Juliette and her new husband with her share of her father's inheritance, properties had to be sold and yet more debts incurred.

When Colette later described Juliette's wedding day, she wrote of how happy she had been, parading around in her pink dress, until she saw her sister, 'trembling

with nerves and raising her unusual mongol-like face towards an unknown man, swooning and submissive to such a point that I felt shame'. Submissiveness was not something Sido had taught her youngest daughter, yet here was Juliette submitting to a man and a family that would become her own family's enemies. The young Colette's sense of independence was, for the first time, being challenged.

As an adult, Colette wrote of how she had treasured the solitude of her childhood days in Saint-Sauveur. She had clung to it and yet she had realised that this solitude would be lost and that her fate as a woman would mean that she too would fall in love. Who can resist the attraction of love? she had asked. 'To become just a woman,' she wrote. 'How paltry and yet how eagerly I pursued that common goal.'

By 1888, when Colette was fifteen, the family was seriously in debt. The final property had been sold and they had only the meagre income from Captain Colette's pension. There were debts they were unable to pay, and the family was once again the butt of sly gossip. A humiliating public auction of their belongings took place, and in 1891 Sido, the Captain and Gabrielle left Saint-Sauveur for nearby Châtillon-sur-Loing (now called Châtillon-Coligny), where Léo and Achille were then both living. Colette never wrote about her departure from Saint-Sauveur; no doubt, the memory of her family's humiliation was too painful.

Achille had set himself up as a doctor in Châtillon-sur-Loing in 1890, after graduating from medical studies in Paris. In 1898, he married Jeanne de la Fare, the daughter of a local family of some note. They had two daughters, Geneviève and Colette, who were the delight of Sido during the last years of her life.

Léo was working in Châtillon as a notary's clerk, but he remained a lost soul, a dreamer who could never let go of his childhood. He later moved to an outer suburb in Paris, where he continued to work as a clerk and harboured a hopeless love for the girlfriend of one of his neighbours. Whenever he came to visit Colette in Paris, it was to talk about Saint-Sauveur and their childhood memories. He regularly went back to Saint-Sauveur, and to Châtillon to visit his mother and his older brother's family. As the years passed, he became more and more disconnected from the realities of life. His only remaining passion was his stamp collection. He died in 1940 at the age of seventy-two, having left Paris for Bléneau in the Yonne *département*, where he was cared for by Achille's daughter Geneviève.

Juliette's was not a happy marriage. Sido's letters to Colette tell of her distress at her eldest child's unhappiness and of her death in 1908, which was followed by an immediate and total rupture with Juliette's surviving husband and daughter.

Colette at 10 years of age

Captain Colette died in 1905. Many years later, Colette, who had no belief in the after life, was taken by a friend to visit a soothsayer. She was told that her father's spirit was looking over her, because she had become the writer he had wanted to be. Like so many children who regretfully mourn for their parents once they are gone, Colette lamented that she had not taken the time to know her father better.

⅋

Colette's childhood home was not sold at auction, but remained the property of Achille, as part of his share of the inheritance. Some years after Achille's death, the house was sold to a silk merchant and his wife, both great admirers of Colette's work. The following year they granted Colette a life interest in the house. It was not until 1950, just a few years before her death, that Colette and her benefactors decided to sell the house to a doctor and his family who had been renting it since 1946.

I have been back to Saint-Sauveur a couple of times since I first started working on this book. On my first return visit, I contacted Samia Bordji, who runs the Colette Study Centre. Yes, she would be delighted to meet me at Saint-Sauveur and show me around the museum devoted to Colette. I was very keen to see the museum, which I knew was housed in the old castle at the top of the village.

The story of the castle is full of the sort of venom on which Saint-Sauveur seemed to thrive. It had belonged to Victor Gandrille, a cousin of Sido's first husband. Gandrille aspired to be mayor of Saint-Sauveur, but his fellow citizens did not share his dream. He was never elected. When he died in 1879, the village felt his vengeance—he left his significant estates to the various municipalities in the region, with the exception of Saint-Sauveur. One of the conditions of his legacy was that the castle was to be maintained as a home for old people—and, to add insult to injury, no inhabitant of Saint-Sauveur was to be admitted.

The museum that is now housed in the castle has a protracted history. Colette de Jouvenel, Colette's daughter, had long-nurtured the idea of setting up a museum in honour of her mother. She had originally wanted the museum to be in Colette's former home in the Palais-Royal, but it had proved to be impossible to buy back the apartment which had, through Colette's will, gone to her last husband and had subsequently been sold. Colette's daughter then turned her attention to the house in Saint-Sauveur, but this too was not for sale. Finally, with the support of the municipality, she worked towards the establishment of a museum in the old castle, which was abandoned and in a poor state of repair.

When Colette de Jouvenel died in 1981, there was still no museum. The cause was taken up by her half-brother, her niece and her nephews. In 1987, they offered to the municipality the collection of material they had inherited from Colette's daughter, which consisted of furniture, books and other objects that had been part of Colette's life, on the condition that a museum be established in the castle. The restoration and installation work took some years and finally, in 1995, the museum was opened. How sad, I thought, that Colette's daughter didn't live to see her work finally come to fruition.

The castle dates from the seventeenth century and was originally set high above the village, which has now grown up around it. It looks out over what used to be a fine park, designed in the French style, but is now rather bare and nondescript. To one side of the building, the old 'saracen' tower still stands, still crumbling away and covered with dense ivy, just as Colette had recalled it.

The steps leading up to the castle are flanked by two stone lions, and the front door opens onto a wide entrance hall and fine staircase. As I walked up the staircase, each step of which bears the name of one of Colette's works, my gaze was transfixed by a photo of Colette projected onto the wall in front of me. Those beautiful soulful eyes never lost their firm gaze, never lost their ability to see the world around her in all its infinite detail.

As Samia showed me through the museum and we talked about the other work being undertaken in the field of Colette studies, I realised I had some catching up to do. A lot had happened in the intervening years, and what was opening up before me promised to be a fascinating journey.

If I had need of any further encouragement, it was there in the museum—a moving portrayal of Colette's life and work, told through images and objects. Rooms from her final residence in the Palais-Royal had been re-created using some of her original furniture. Her collection of glass paperweights with their captured kaleidoscope of colour and pattern, her butterfly collection, her botanical books with their delicate illustrations that were always within her reach, the chipped blue ceramic pot with her collection of thick Parker pens—all these objects accompanied Colette from one residence to the next, and are as familiar to her readers as they were to her. There were portraits and photographs, postcards and letters. Her gravelly voice, with its rolled 'r's and its musical rhythm, accompanied me as I wandered through the rooms. On the top floor, a documentary film brought Colette to life in front of my eyes. It was as though Colette was there, speaking to me, across the years.

From a second-floor window, I looked down on the village and into the garden of the house where Colette was born, the childhood paradise, with all its memories, that was left behind when Colette and her parents set off from Saint-Sauveur for nearby Châtillon.

I can still see it all before my eyes, the garden with its warm walls, the last dark cherries hanging on the tree, the sky webbed with long pink clouds ... If I so choose, the wind rustles the stiff papery bamboo and sings in thousands of streams of parted air through the combs of the yew tree.

Illustration by Grau Sala for La Maison de Claudine

Chapter 2

— Childhood paradise — lost and regained —

The house and garden still live on but what does it matter if the magic has left them, if the secret is lost that once opened—light, smells, harmony of trees and birds, murmuring of human voices stayed by death—onto a world of which I am no longer worthy?

In Châtillon-sur-Loing, Colette's life was to change. She was now aged almost nineteen. At school in Saint-Sauveur, she had been a bright and quick student, though somewhat mischievous. She had always gained excellent marks in French, but was somewhat less gifted in science. Having gained her secondary school certificate, Colette was encouraged by her headmistress, Mademoiselle Terrain, to go on to study for her higher-level certificate. But the family's move to Châtillon in 1891 put an end to that.

The family's departure from Saint-Sauveur may have been ignominious but they were well received in Châtillon. Achille was highly respected as a doctor and was to marry well. From time to time, Colette would accompany him on his rounds, but there was little to interest her in Châtillon and the days must have passed very slowly for her.

What did the future offer a young woman in a small country town? Marriage, spinsterhood, teaching—there were not many options, and without a dowry, where would she find a husband? Chance, however, was to play its part, bringing to Châtillon the son of an old acquaintance of Captain Colette.

Henri Gauthier-Villars was the son of Jean-Albert Gauthier-Villars, who ran a successful scientific publishing house in Paris. Henri was born in 1859 in Villiers-sur-Orge, on the outskirts of the capital. After completing his studies at the École Polytechnique in Paris, he joined his father's publishing house. Henri, who by affectation changed the spelling of his name to Henry, was more interested in music and literature than in the sciences. Under various pseudonyms—Willy, the Usherette at the Summer Circus, Maugis—he wrote and published musical criticism, poetry and popular novels.

Willy, as he became known, had a taste for the ladies, and had fallen in love with a married woman. In 1889 he was living with her in Paris before she had obtained a divorce from her husband. They had a son, Jacques, to whom Willy gave his name, Gauthier-Villars. Two years later, the boy's mother fell seriously ill and died. The baby had to be entrusted to a foster mother and it was to Châtillon, and his father's friends, that Willy turned. Achille, as the doctor in the town, was responsible for

Colette on the banks of the River Loing

the care of children put into foster care. Little Jacques was in Châtillon for about six months—enough time for Willy, on his regular visits, to become susceptible to the charms of the young Colette, even though he was mourning the death of the woman he had loved.

Sido was anxious to make the most of this possibility of marriage, and arranged for Colette to visit Paris. A flirtatious relationship developed, with Willy taking the 19-year-old girl to the theatre and to dinner. Other visits to Paris followed, and Willy continued to be a regular visitor to Châtillon after his parents assumed the care of his son. By the end of 1892, against the wishes of Willy's parents, who had envisaged a marriage to someone who would bring a significant dowry, Colette and Willy were officially engaged.

Although captivated by Colette's lively spirit and beauty, Willy was less than enthusiastic about the marriage. In a letter to his younger brother, he wrote that he was marrying out of a sense of gratitude to the family that had been so kind to his son. Compromised by his romantic affairs and the existence of a son born out of wedlock, Willy had limited options.

For Colette, Willy offered an escape from Châtillon and from the spinsterhood that awaited girls without a dowry. Moreover, Colette was in love. She had fallen for this man from the capital, who wrote her witty and ardent letters.

In May 1893, when she was just twenty, Sidonie-Gabrielle Colette married Henri Gauthier-Villars in a simple ceremony in Châtillon. The Gauthier-Villars family did not attend, and Willy had just two friends as his witnesses. There was no wedding feast, just a simple family meal. The following day, the couple left Châtillon for Paris. Colette was leaving behind her childhood, her family and her birthplace. She would not return in search of her past for many years.

After the death of Captain Colette in 1905, Sido lived on alone in Châtillon for a further seven years. Colette's visits to her mother were few and far between, despite the letters that constantly entreated her to come. Once Colette had broken free of the magic circle of Sido's love, it was as though she no longer wanted to be part of it. She wrote that she initially feared going back to visit because she knew that her mother would want to tuck her into bed as she had done when she was a child, and have long heart-to-heart talks.

As the years went on, however, it was the pace of her own life that kept Colette away. With her career on the stage and her journalism, she had many other demands on her time, and Sido made it very clear in her letters that she did not approve of these occupations. To her mind they were distracting her daughter from her real vocation as a serious writer.

Sido's letters reveal a very deep mother's love. Colette was always her 'golden sunshine' whose presence brightened a room. But her letters also hint at another side to her character, for Sido was dominating and possessive, to the point that she confused her daughter's persona with her own. 'You are me,' she declared. She was furious when Colette had her long braids cut off. 'Your hair was not yours to cut,' she wrote, 'it was my work of art.' She complained that her daughter visited other people, and travelled to all sorts of places, but couldn't find the time to visit her.

Colette could never become her own person without escaping from the demands of her mother, so she visited rarely and her ageing mother had to content herself with letters and postcards, gifts of the little luxuries she liked—her favourite tea, chocolates, flowers, fruit, fine woollen stockings—and the money that was Colette's regular contribution to her mother's keep.

The years passed and the correspondence continued. Finally, after many a broken promise, Colette went to see her mother for a couple of days in August 1912. She was only able to spare a few days from her busy schedule and the emotional turmoil of the early days of her relationship with the man who was to become her second husband. Sido died just a few weeks later on 25 September 1912, at the age of seventy-seven.

Colette did not attend the funeral, nor did she wear mourning. She was interested in life, not death, as indeed Sido had been, and she did not want to share her sorrow in a public display of mourning. Besides, it was not convenient for her to leave Paris, as she was performing in a new mime drama, *The Night Bird*.

Just occasionally, however, Colette let her guard drop. Ten years after her mother's death, she wrote to her life-long friend Marguerite Moreno that she had just chanced upon a letter from her mother, written towards the end of her life, 'written in pencil, with half-finished words and already full of her imminent departure'.

How curious it is. You bravely resist tears, you hold yourself together at the toughest of times. And then someone waves at you from behind a window, you come across an open flower that was closed the day before, a letter falls out of a drawer, and everything comes crashing down around you.

Colette when she was fifteen years old, with long braids

Colette's process of mourning was private. It meant coming to terms with her own womanhood, finding her own path and letting go of the child in her, the child who always sought a dominant figure in her intimate relations. It is perhaps not insignificant that Colette's only child was conceived shortly after Sido's death, when Colette was almost forty.

From her mother, Colette had learnt a proud independence of spirit, a quick-wittedness and sense of her own value. Sido had been a strong and dominating mother, whose love had been both a burden and a joy. While Colette succeeded in breaking free of Sido's possessive, overpowering love, Achille never did. He remained tied to his mother emotionally and physically, through the routine of his daily visits. Indeed, he did not outlast her long, dying just a year after her death. He never forgave Colette for not coming to their mother's funeral and he burnt all her letters to Sido. Tantalisingly, all that remains of this correspondence are the letters from Sido to Colette, and just a few postcards from Colette.

'Yes, yes, you love me,' Sido wrote to Colette, 'but you are a daughter, a female animal, my likeness and my rival.' You will miss me when I am gone, she acutely observed, but you will not suffer in the way Achille will. 'For you, it won't be a big thing. You have escaped, you have set up your nest far from me.'

Colette had indeed thrown off the yoke of a mother's imprisoning love to become her own person, but she had not escaped her influence. 'I have never taken leave of a character who slowly has imposed herself on all my work,' she wrote. She would throw off other yokes as she followed her path towards being a free and liberated woman, but as she did with Sido, she would appropriate them for her own literary purposes.

It was only after she had reached her own maturity that Colette was able to look back and pay homage to her mother. As she herself wrote, 'It takes time for the absent one to take shape within our minds.'

❧

Ten years after Sido's death, and twenty years after she had left the house and garden in Saint-Sauveur, Colette turned her gaze back to her childhood, to the village where she was born, and placed her mother at the centre of the childhood paradise that we know through her books. With *La Maison de Claudine*, published in 1921, and *Sido*, published seven years later, the myth of Sido as the goddess mother became central to Colette's creation of her own mythology, of the poetic reality she would continue to build through her work. Sido became the legendary figure who drew sustenance from the earth, who communicated with nature, who opened her house towards those who were weak or in need, who despised petty-mindedness and righteousness.

'Sido and my childhood, one and the other, one by the other, were happy in the middle of an imaginary eight-pointed star,' Colette wrote, coming back time and again to Saint-Sauveur and the image of her mother as the central point of a weathervane, which in French is called *la rose des vents* ('the rose of the winds').

Today, Saint-Sauveur is Colette country. The steep street with the house where she was born has been renamed rue Colette. Little else, however, has changed. In 2011, on my last visit to the village, it had a somewhat deserted air. The squat church at the bottom of the village was firmly shut. The *bar-tabac* was also closed, and the bakery was about to pull down its shutters. It was one o'clock and there was no one in the streets. Quickly, we needed to buy something to eat.

My partner and I were staying in a bed and breakfast run by a friendly Englishwoman and her French husband. They were tree-changers, having left Paris for the quiet life in a little country village. They had a large rambling garden in front of their house and we sat in the sun, enjoying a cup of tea and our little quiches from the bakery. Some scenes for a recent film about Colette and her life in the village had been filmed in this very garden, and the owners had become involved in various activities of the Society of Friends of Colette, including the campaign to purchase the house where Colette was born. The house had been on the market for a couple of years and an international effort had been mounted to raise funds for its purchase.

The campaign was successful, and the house now belongs to the society. Work has begun to re-create the house and garden of Colette's childhood as a study centre and place for people to visit. In the meantime, the house and its garden and the surrounding countryside live on in the imagination of all her readers, as they did in Colette's own memory.

Pray, give me, the better to entice you, give me pastel crayons, of colours as yet without names, give me sparkling powders and a fairy brush, and … Well, no, for there are no words, no crayons, no colours that could paint for you, above a mauve slate roof adorned with russet mosses, the sky of my homeland, as it beamed down upon my childhood!

Chapter 3
— Marriage and Belle Époque Paris —

*T*he only danger that came my way, in rue Jacob, was the attraction of shadows, the temptation of a cloistered life. I caught a glimpse of the seduction of all that is dark, confined, made for motionless revelry, and, in contempt of my youth, I was only interested in brief intervals of fresh air, a little gust of spring hail rushing in through the open window, the faint perfume of invisible lilac, rising up from a nearby garden.

It is hard to imagine this bright and lively young woman being tempted by the shadows of a life in a dark and airless space. Yet the photos of Colette at this time exude a heaviness of heart and melancholy that seem to reflect these dark and soulless interiors.

Paris in the 1890s was an elegant, hedonistic city with a dynamic intellectual, social and artistic life. Haussmann's urban redevelopment had created the city as we know it today—with its wide tree-lined avenues, its long vistas ending in grand buildings, the elegant department stores, its public gardens. Cabaret, dance, music and theatre attracted Parisians and visitors from around the world alike. The new opera house, the Palais Garnier, had opened in 1875 and was a magnet for Parisian social life. The Folies Bergère was in full swing and the Moulin Rouge had opened in 1889. The impressionists had transformed the visual arts, and Art Nouveau was creating a new aesthetic for architecture and the decorative arts. It was the age of the cancan and of the great courtesans, Liane de Pougy and Caroline Otéro, a time when life was lived on the boulevards—in the cafes and restaurants, the theatres and opera—and in the salons of the great hostesses of the time.

It was Paris of the Belle Époque, a period of peace and prosperity that was to last to the First World War. The sense of optimism was exemplified in the great Universal Exhibition of 1889, and symbolised visually in the Eiffel Tower, which was built for the exhibition. The 1900 Universal Exhibition would also leave its mark on Paris as we know it today, in two imposing structures—the Grand Palais and the Petit Palais—and in the Paris *métro*, its entrances graced by Hector Guimard's sinuous Art Nouveau designs.

This was the city where Colette found herself in 1893, as the newly married wife of Willy. She was twenty; he was thirty-four, a Parisian rake, writer, music critic, man about town, who knew everyone and was invited everywhere. The life of the newlyweds was a whirlwind of opening nights, concerts and fashionable salons.

For a number of years, Colette and Willy were regulars at the salons of Madame Arman de Caillavet, the Princesse Edmond de Polignac (Winnaretta Singer), and the publisher Alfred Vallette and his wife Rachilde, who was herself a writer. Madame de Caillavet received the leaders of Parisian literary society: Anatole France was her lover, Marcel Proust was a very close friend of her son Gaston and was often in attendance. Indeed, Madame de Caillavet was the model for certain aspects of the character of Madame Verdurin in Proust's *Remembrance of Things Past*, particularly her somewhat imperious manner. Others whom Colette would have met there included the French aesthete Robert de Montesquiou—another model for one of Proust's characters—the countess and poet Anna de Noailles, the great actress Sarah Bernhardt, and the prince and princess Bibesco. All of these people would re-emerge in Colette's life at different times.

Colette quickly developed close friendships with the writer Marcel Schwob and with Paul Masson, both of whom were friends of Willy. Schwob's literary works stand beside those of the great symbolists of the time, and he was also renowned as an Orientalist and translator. He would often visit Colette, carrying with him a volume of short stories or a novel by an English or American writer—Robert Louis Stevenson, Mark Twain, Dickens or Daniel Defoe—that he hadn't yet translated but that he would read to her, translating as he went. It was through Schwob, who

Illustration by André Dignimont for Claudine à Paris

died in 1905 when he was just thirty-seven, that Colette met the actress Marguerite Moreno, whom he married in 1900. The two women quickly established a friendship that lasted until Moreno's death in 1948.

Moreno recalled her first meeting with Colette in the couple's dark and depressing Paris apartment: 'When I first met you, Colette, you lived in an "almost" old building in rue Jacob. It had a gloomy courtyard, the staircase was vast and cold … You were reading. Your long plait of hair was wound around you like a serpent and you turned your face towards me—a face that has only changed by becoming more beautiful as you have profited from life. At that time, life was refusing you many things!'

Paul Masson was an older man. His interest in Colette gave her confidence in those very qualities that made her different from other young women. Masson had travelled, and had been a magistrate in Chandannagar in West Bengal. When Colette knew him, he worked as a cataloguer at the Bibliothèque nationale. But Masson wasn't satisfied with cataloguing what was in the collection—he preferred to focus on what was missing. Having noticed that there were significant gaps in the collection, he filled them with the 'titles of extremely interesting works that should have been written'. But, Colette asked, what about the books? Are you going to write them? 'Oh,' he replied with a frivolous gesture, 'I can't do everything!'

It was surely Colette's gamin nature, her unconventionality, her intelligence and wit, and perhaps her melancholy, that attracted the attention and friendship of these idiosyncratic, whimsical and highly intelligent men.

Through Willy, Colette also met a number of musicians. Willy wrote a regular music column and was an avid supporter of Wagner and many of the emerging French composers—Vincent d'Indy, Debussy, Chabrier and Chausson. In her *Journal à rebours* (*Looking Backwards*), Colette recalled her first meeting with Maurice Ravel, at the salon of Madame de Saint-Marceaux, where musicians and music lovers gathered on Friday evenings. One evening, the young Ravel arrived, timid, a bit distant. Colette was enchanted by his music, which was at once sensual and somewhat mischievous. Many years later, their paths would cross again when Colette was invited to write a libretto for an opera-ballet. She enthusiastically agreed when Ravel was proposed as the composer. The result was *L'Enfant et les sortilèges* (*The Child and the Magic Spells*). While Colette wrote the libretto in just a few days in 1916, it took Ravel many years to complete the music. He had been drafted into the army during the First World War, and had seen a great deal of death. He was also mourning his mother, and had fallen into a state of despair. It wasn't until 1920 that he took up work on the opera, which was finally premiered in Monte Carlo in 1925 by the Monte Carlo Opera Company and Ballet, with choreography by George Balanchine.

Debussy was another favourite. Colette wrote a delightful piece about the composer in 1923 for the newspaper *Le Matin*, which was included in her 1950 collection *Trait pour trait*. In it, she remembered an evening after they had attended the first performance in Paris of one of Rimsky-Korsakov's works. Was it *Antar* or *Scheherazade*, she tried to recall. Debussy hummed the tunes, trying to re-create from his memory the melodic line. Someone else picked it up, and Debussy, using his hands, his feet, his arms and his voice, channelled the sounds of violins, cellos, tympani and xylophone, becoming the image of a dancing, laughing faun.

In spite of this constant round of activities, Colette was lonely and disillusioned. Willy was out from morning to late at night, and she spent many hours alone in their sunless apartment, a home that she suspected had 'stifled too many souls'. Looking back, when she wrote about this period of her life, she couldn't remember doing anything other than wait. 'For the person who is waiting, no other occupation is necessary,' she wrote.

Colette reflected that she led a rather modest life during the first year of her marriage. She would go out for breakfast with Willy, and then he would be off on his business and she would return to the apartment, where she would spend the day by herself, with occasional visits from her new friends, waiting for Willy to come home and whisk her off to whatever dinner or performance or salon was happening. Colette found herself longing for this city life to end and to find herself transported back to the house and garden where she had grown up. Her health was being jeopardised; she was eating badly, nibbling on sweets rather than eating regular meals. She was soon to be pushed further into despair.

Marriage had not presented any obstacle to Willy's philandering. He continued to have affairs, and the gossips in Paris ensured that Colette knew about them. Warned by an anonymous letter, Colette put on her coat and set off one day to an unknown address, where she found Willy with his mistress. What shocked her more than anything was that she found them not in bed, but bent over a book of accounts. This seems so improbable that it may well have been the truth, although the book in which she recounted her memories of this period, *Mes apprentissages* (*My Apprenticeships*), was written many years later, and was a somewhat embittered point-scoring exercise against her first husband.

By mid-1894, Colette had fallen into a deep state of despondency and was seriously

ill. She seemed to have lost all taste for life. Over the next few months, she was slowly nursed back to health by her mother, who hurried to her daughter's side, as well as by her dear friends Masson and Schwob. Madame Arman de Caillavet, who had been quite taken by this young woman from the provinces, would bring special treats—a pineapple, peaches—and her bossy voice and outrageous perfume acted as a tonic for Colette. Two months' convalescence at Belle-Île-en-Mer in Brittany— accompanied by Willy for some of the time and, in his absence, by Paul Masson— completed her recuperation.

Colette returned to Paris with the realisation that in order to survive, she needed to toughen up and make the most of her situation, rather than be a victim of it. It was time 'neither to die for someone else, nor because of someone else', a lesson that was to stand her in good stead throughout her life.

❧

Today, the rue Jacob, just off the boulevard Saint-Germain, is a street of small, elegant shops, boutique hotels and restaurants. The apartment building where Colette lived, number 28, has been renovated. There is a plaque on the front of the building, with the familiar Colette signature. Colette lived here, it reads, during the first years of her literary life in Paris, from 1893 to 1896.

Like so much of Paris, this area has lost the slightly seedy, run-down character that I recall from the early 1970s. These narrow streets between the boulevard Saint-Germain and the river were the haunts of artists and art students, of cheap little hotels where writers, artists and musicians could afford to live. The hotel where Oscar Wilde passed the last few years of his life has been completely renovated, and is now an extremely upmarket, chic establishment. Many of the small publishing houses, bookshops and artist-supply stores have given way to luxury brand names, and expensive design and interior decorating shops.

However, the past is still present. Just next door to 28 rue Jacob is a bookshop that would definitely have met with Colette's approval: La Maison Rustique, founded in 1836, its display window full of the most enticing books on gardens and plants. Opposite is a little shop crammed with furniture, lamps and richly coloured table settings in shapes and designs that would have appealed to Colette.

Next door to the furniture store is a dealer in manuscripts and photographs. I went in to see if the owner had anything relating to Colette, as letters and postcards still appear in auction houses and in private sales. He showed me a very handsome photograph of Colette by Germaine Krull, dating from 1936, as well as a small display window with other pieces—a manuscript of one of her essays, a few postcards, a couple of smaller familiar photos. Regrettably, all were well beyond my budget. The owner of the shop was fascinated to learn that Colette had lived in this street. He had never noticed the plaque.

I walked further along rue Jacob to number 20, where Natalie Clifford Barney, a wealthy American heiress, held her famous Friday salons. She settled in Paris in 1902, and from 1909 until the 1960s she rented the two-storey villa in the courtyard of 20 rue Jacob, with its garden and famous Temple of Friendship. This was surely the garden that Colette could just see from her window at number 28.

Clifford Barney's Friday salons became the centre of an international literary and lesbian society. The poet Renée Vivien, artist Romaine Brooks and writer Djuna Barnes were all part of her close circle. Her love affairs were legendary—with the great courtesan Liane de Pougy, with Renée Vivien, with Romaine Brooks … and with Colette. The two women maintained a close friendship until Colette's death.

Behind the firmly closed entrance door, there are still some vestiges of the garden where Miss Barney, or l'Amazone, as she was known, entertained her guests with tableaux and dances, in which Colette occasionally appeared. In a series of sketches of women writers of the period, Natalie Clifford Barney recalled that it was at her salon that Colette premiered scenes from the theatrical adaptation of her novel *La Vagabonde*, with Marguerite Moreno and the couturier Paul Poiret performing with her.

In spite of how it has changed over the years, Saint-Germain is still one of my favourite *quartiers* in Paris. I love to have a morning coffee and croissant at the Café de Flore. The regulars are still there—different from the cafe's clientele in the heyday of the 1920s to 1940s, and certainly different from when Colette lived in this neighbourhood. But there is a sense of the unchanging nature of the rhythm of the city as I sit and watch the young mothers walking their children to school, the shop assistants hurrying from the *métro*, the older retired gentlemen coming into the cafe and taking their regular places, with a nod to the

waiter who, as he brings their newspaper and coffee and places the basket of brioches and croissants on their table, exchanges a few brief words about the state of the world. It is a comfortable and comforting routine.

Neither of the Left Bank cafes frequented by Colette still exists. The Café d'Harcourt on the place de la Sorbonne was a favourite meeting place for younger writers, as was the Café Vachette on the corner of boulevard Saint-Michel and rue des Écoles. Here, Colette enjoyed spending time with a younger crowd than the habitués of the Right Bank cafes favoured by Willy. The Vachette was the first to go—in 1913, torn down to make way for a bank. The d'Harcourt was closed down by the German occupying forces in 1940. It was a favourite haunt of students, and the Germans responded to a minor student revolt by turning it into a bookstore that sold German and collaborationist literature. Needless to say, the bookstore was not well patronised. The cafe didn't reopen after the war.

In late 1896, Willy and Colette left the Left Bank to take up residence in what were known as the *beaux quartiers*, over on the Right Bank, beyond the place des Ternes. Their first move was to an artist's studio on the sixth floor of 93 rue de Courcelles, and then, in 1902, to an apartment at 177 *bis*, in the same street. 'A bourgeois threat emanated from every corner at 177 *bis*,' Colette wrote, and indeed the area still has a very bourgeois air today, apparently barely changed from when Colette lived there. Number 177 has been replaced by an ugly building that dates from the 1960s or '70s, but 93 rue de Courcelles remains intact, with a fine polished wooden door and attractive cast-iron balconies on the first floor, in typical Haussmann style. On the street level is a boutique of the famous French *perfumier* Annick Goutal.

Not far from rue de Courcelles is Parc Monceau, a haven of 19th-century tranquillity and elegance in a Paris that can at times seem to be totally dominated by motor vehicles. Colette does not mention it, but she surely would have taken her little bulldog, Toby-Chien, for walks there.

It was after the recovery of her health and the return from Belle-Île-en-Mer that Colette made her literary debut, writing a number of articles about music for a short-lived review, *La Cocarde*. All six articles were signed Colette Gauthier-Villars. Then, in the summer of 1895, Colette and Willy returned to Saint-Sauveur as guests of honour at the school's prize-giving ceremony. It was perhaps this trip, when they had stayed in the girls' dormitory, that prompted Willy to suggest that Colette should

The Claudine *novels, Willy and Colette and Polaire*

jot down some of the schoolgirl memories she had recounted to him.

Willy had a considerable stable of ghostwriters working for him, his first novel having emerged from this stable in 1894. With funds low, he perhaps thought he might be able to make something out of his wife's recollections of her schooldays. So Colette bought herself a number of notebooks, just like she had used at school, and started to write, creating the character of Claudine, her first literary alter ego. She was 'just like me before my marriage', she wrote to Mademoiselle Terrain, her school headmistress, 'perhaps worse, more disorderly, more dotty, more ill-mannered, and prettier'. Some months later, Colette handed the notebooks to Willy who, after taking a cursory look at them, decided the work was not publishable and stuffed them into a drawer.

Four years later, Willy came across the notebooks when he was tidying his desk and realised his error. What a fool, he muttered and, gathering up the notebooks, he grabbed his top hat and raced out the door to his publisher. The manuscript needed a bit of spicing up, but it was publishable. So, as Colette later wrote, she set to work again, following Willy's suggestions, adding jokes, puns, some local slang and a bit of naughtiness.

The extent of Willy's involvement in the birth of *Claudine* is unknown, as none of the various versions of the manuscript have survived. Certainly, it was highly likely that the manuscript was given the same treatment as others emerging from Willy's stable, and was reworked by one of Willy's collaborators or by Willy himself. What is undeniable is that when *Claudine à l'école* (*Claudine at School*) finally appeared in 1900, it was an instant success. Within just a few months it had sold forty thousand copies.

The book was published under Willy's name, and Willy was quick to maximise the opportunity presented by its success. A sequel, *Claudine à Paris*, was published in 1901, with *Claudine en ménage* (*Claudine Married*) following in 1902 and the last in the series, *Claudine s'en va* (*Claudine and Annie*), in 1903.

Looking back on these *Claudine* novels, Colette was not particularly proud of them. They had a certain youthful freshness, but they were tainted by a lack of discretion and a careless disregard for hurting people.

While Colette drew on her memories of her childhood in Saint-Sauveur, Claudine is not the young Colette and the character's home in Montigny is not Saint-Sauveur. Claudine is motherless. She lives in the little village of Montigny with her vague and distracted father, and has all the characteristics of a young girl untrammelled by motherly love and guidance. Truth and fiction collide nonetheless. The school Colette describes in *Claudine à l'école*, rife with lesbian relationships and corruption, is not that of her childhood, but many of the novel's characters are recognisable inhabitants of Saint-Sauveur. Mademoiselle Terrain is caricatured shamelessly, which seems particularly harsh as Colette's headmistress was a woman before her time, not unlike Colette; she had a child, without being married, and lived independently. Many of Colette's schoolfriends, teachers and townsfolk are also targeted. Even the public school system, so dear to Colette's parents' political values, is mercilessly caricatured.

Willy and Colette in the apartment at 177 bis rue de Courcelles

Claudine en ménage (*Claudine Married*) is essentially a roman à clef, caricaturing friends and enemies. Following in the tradition of a number of Willy's previous novels, ghostwritten by other writers in his literary stable, it was based on an episode in Colette's life—a lesbian affair that had been provoked as much by Willy as by Colette's own curiosity.

Rézi, who is a Viennese beauty with whom Claudine has an affair, is modelled on Georgie Raoul-Duval, the daughter of a rich family from Louisiana. In 1891, Georgie had married René Raoul-Duval, the scion of a wealthy and distinguished family. Georgie was an extremely attractive and charming woman, who was also intelligent and cultivated. Willy and Colette had met her in the salon of Madame Jeanne Mühlfeld. The liaison between Colette and Georgie appears to have started around the time of the publication of *Claudine à Paris*, in March 1901, and had come to an end by October. In the summer of that year, Georgie had certainly been in Bayreuth with Colette and Willy, and the relationship had become a threesome. It is very possible that Georgie was already involved with Willy before she started her affair with Colette.

This three-way relationship was the inspiration for the novel, although Colette claimed in a letter to Jeanne Mühlfeld that it was Willy who was transforming her character Rézi into an 'awfully recognisable' Georgie. When Madame Raoul-Duval was warned about the book's imminent publication, she offered the publishing house a considerable sum of money to pulp its print run. However, Willy was not to be deterred and took a slightly revised version of the manuscript to another publishing house, which was happy to run the risk of legal action, and the book was published in the spring of 1902. No legal proceedings eventuated and the book was a *succès de scandale*, with seventy thousand copies printed within just a few months.

Through these *Claudine* novels, Colette was revealing the emergence within herself of what she called 'an agreeable and slow corruptibility', having been introduced to the 'secret of sensual pleasure, which she played with, like a child with a deadly weapon'. She was being seduced by Willy's 'incorrigible frivolity', which diminished everything in life to a futile and harmful game.

Although Willy was named as the author of all four Claudine novels, there were some who guessed that Colette was, in fact, the principal author. The writer Catulle Mendès wrote to her saying that in twenty or thirty years she would be known as the author and that she would realise what it means to have created a 'type' in literature. He described it as being like a sort of punishment that follows you around, clings to you and 'makes you want to vomit'.

From left: Willy and his 'twins' at the races, Polaire, and Polaire, Willy and Colette

Colette had certainly created a 'type', and Willy was quick to profit. He did not hesitate to promote himself as the author of the *Claudine* novels, although he willingly acknowledged his young wife as the source of his inspiration. In 1902, a stage adaptation of the first two books catapulted *Claudine* to celebrity status.

Willy understood the power of theatre. As the critic Edmond de Goncourt had written in 1892, 'if you really want to be known in literature, you have to be on the stage, because the theatre is all the literature a lot of people know'. The theatres of the Paris boulevards were in their heyday, and what was on and who was playing were the topics of conversation in cafes and salons. Within just a few months of the publication of *Claudine à Paris*, the stage adaptation by Willy, written in collaboration with the famous theatre director Aurélien Lugné-Poë and scriptwriter Charles Vayre, was ready to be premiered at the Théâtre des Bouffes-Parisiens. With the young actress Polaire in the role of Claudine, it played for five months and was a huge success.

Polaire was the stage name of a singer and actress who had started her career in the music hall. *Claudine* was her first dramatic role and she became a celebrity, continuing to perform on the stage and in the early film industry until the mid-1930s. She wore her curly hair cropped short around her face, and her dark eye make-up accentuated her pale complexion. She famously had the tiniest of waists, no more than thirty-six centimetres, like a bracelet, Colette wrote.

Colette had grown tired of tying up her heavy weight of hair and, perhaps at Willy's suggestion, she decided to cut her hair short like Polaire's. This was well before it was fashionable for women to have short hair. The resemblance between Polaire and Colette was striking; both of them had shapely figures and, dressed in the matching outfits that Willy bought for them, they looked just like twins.

Willy delighted in escorting his 'twins' around town. They were seen at the races, at the Palais de Glace on the Champs-Élysées, or riding in the Bois de Boulogne. Polaire tolerated this exhibitionism reluctantly, writing later that she felt humiliated being paraded around Paris with Colette like a couple of Great Danes. Colette was more sanguine. Ten years of living with Willy had given her a tougher skin, and she was not going to show her humiliation in public. She was learning to hide her private feelings behind the mask of her public persona.

The opportunity to profit further from the success of *Claudine* did not escape Willy, and a profusion of products appeared on the market. Claudine collars became fashionable. A well-known milliner created a Claudine hat. Lotions, perfume, postcards, cigarettes—all appeared bearing the famous name. Even a Claudine ice cream and Claudine cake appeared in the window of one of Paris's famous pastry shops.

Willy was also a master of self-promotion and the *Claudine* novels contained a devastatingly accurate portrait of him in the character of Maugis, who made his first appearance in *Claudine à Paris*. Maugis was pure Willy and he would appear in many other works from the Willy stable. He was Willy's creation and, in creating him, Colette was later to write, Willy had yielded to his megalomania, his obsession with painting his own portrait, his love of self-regard.

A decade after her arrival in Paris, Colette was no longer an unknown young girl from the provinces. She was sought out for her originality, her lively and sharp wit, her spontaneity, and she had a wide circle of friends. She was recognised in her own right as a modern young woman, even if her fate still seemed strongly linked to that of Willy, who was in many ways being left behind by the social changes that were taking place in France.

The Dreyfus affair had sharply divided French society in the final years of the nineteenth century. Captain Dreyfus, of Jewish descent, had been condemned for treason. When evidence appeared that he had been framed, he was retried and, on the basis of further false evidence, was again convicted. Parisian society was divided into those who supported Dreyfus's innocence and those who condemned him. Zola's famous pamphlet, *J'accuse*, in support of Dreyfus, was published in 1898. Finally, in 1906, Dreyfus was exonerated and reinstated in the French Army.

Willy had positioned himself with those who were anti-Dreyfus. He was anti-Semitic, and had no hesitation in making his opinions known through his articles. With the literary and intellectual avant-garde supporting Dreyfus's innocence, Willy was squarely in the camp of the intellectual conservatives, in spite of his ardent support for what was new in music.

Colette's position was less overt. Anti-Semitism ran deep in French society and Colette was certainly not immune to it, even though she was later to marry a man of Jewish descent. In spite of her father's political aspirations and her mother's liberal social values, she was never interested in politics and she did not espouse any political position. For her, the personal was certainly not political, as it was for so many other women writers. She wrote about the difficulties women faced in leading independent lives, she was committed to individual freedom and to not being constrained by society's norms, but she was never to turn these issues into a political ethic. Politically complacent from these early years, her guiding moral compass seemed to derive primarily from her growing awareness that one is wholly responsible for one's own wellbeing. She had a strong sense of self-preservation, and though she respected and valued other people, she would always put her own interests first. Clearly, she was not likely to join the forces of those who were publicly protesting Dreyfus's innocence. What she thought privately, we will never know.

By 1904, Colette had written four novels, all of which had appeared under Willy's name. She was still in search of her own personal style, but was becoming increasingly aware of her talents as a writer. Now thirty-one years old, she was beginning to test her abilities in new ways. She had a gymnasium installed in the apartment, and began to train her body for the freedom and independence she aspired to. It was as though she had decided that by freeing her body, she would free herself.

Colette was learning a new trade—to be a mime and dancer—new skills that would provide her with other ways of earning her living. From the time of her parents' financial losses and the enforced departure from her childhood home and garden, financial insecurity was a spectre that hung over her life. The need to earn money, to ensure her financial independence, was never far from her thoughts throughout her life. Willy was a spendthrift and a gambler, and was constantly in debt. This, possibly more than his mistresses, was the cause of the final rupture between them.

Colette had thought of leaving the marriage, but she had made no move. Where would she go, and how would she survive? She owned nothing in her own right— not even the books she had written—and she was still in love with Willy. According to Colette, after twelve years of marriage, it was Willy who made the first move. Willy's version was different: it was Colette who left. What we can assume to be the truth is that each was looking for a way out as they explored new relationships.

Willy's latest mistress was a younger woman, Marguerite Maniez, known as Meg

Villars. Born in London in 1885 to French parents, she had been brought up in England. She was one of many young women who, having read the *Claudine* novels, threw themselves at Willy, but this relationship was assuming much greater importance than many of Willy's other dalliances.

At the same time, Colette was being courted by Missy, the Marquise de Belbeuf, and in the summer of 1906 they holidayed at Le Crotoy on the Picardy coast. By the end of the summer, Colette and Willy were both back in Paris, but living separately, Colette in a little ground-floor apartment on the rue de Villejust, now the rue Paul-Valéry, in the 16th arrondissement. She realised that her life was about to change in just the same way that 'the bouquet of a wine changes according to which side of the slope the grapes are grown'.

The building no longer exists—it was pulled down just a couple of years later to make way for a modern apartment block—but this ground-floor flat, full of light and sunshine, was a charming abode where Colette, living by herself for the first time, found happiness and security. Close to the Bois de Boulogne, she could watch the horseriders passing by, breathe in the fresh air of the park, its 'perfume of catalpa in springtime and its yellow aroma of fallen leaves in autumn'.

There would be many more moves within Paris over the next thirty years and, with each move, Colette appropriated another part of the city—the village-like atmosphere of Auteuil, the grand vistas of the Champs-Élysées, the bourgeois surroundings of the 8th arrondissement and, finally, the village within a city, the Palais-Royal. After one of her many moves, she wrote to Marguerite Moreno that 'when an abode has rendered up its juices, it is time to leave … creatures like us are enriched each time we change our surroundings'. Through a succession of twelve moves over forty-five years, Colette remained faithful to Paris and to what she called its 'provincial alluvial deposits'.

Paris provided the backdrop for many of her works. Her experiences of Paris at the turn of the century, its social life, the salons, restaurants and theatres, the

demi-monde of courtesans, the lesbian circles and the bohemian life of artists and performers—they all inspired much of her fiction, short stories, chronicles and journalism, The locations are unmistakably Parisian—the Bois de Boulogne, where Renée in *La Vagabonde* (*The Vagabond*) takes her little dog Fossette for a run every Sunday, and where 'from the bare lawns there arises a trembling, silvery incense, that smells of mushroom'; the boudoir of Léa in *Chéri*; the small apartment belonging to Madame Alvarez in *Gigi*, where she lives with her daughter and granddaughter, and which provides a welcome respite from fashionable Paris for the wealthy Gaston, whose love affairs the women follow with interest in the daily gossip rag, *Gil Blas*.

Today, a visit to Maxim's on the rue Royale is one way to recapture the Paris of the time. The restaurant was established in 1893 and, under its second owner, who gave the dining room its celebrated Art Nouveau décor, it became one of Paris's most fashionable places to dine. The magnificent location provided the setting for scenes in two films based on Colette's novels—*Gigi* and *Chéri*. In 1981, Pierre Cardin bought Maxim's and established a museum on the upper floors of the building to house his outstanding collection of Art Nouveau furniture and objects. The museum is set up like the apartment of a courtesan, where it is easy to imagine Léa and Chéri having lunch at the dining table set with fine silver and delicate pink plates.

As the Belle Époque was drawing to a close, Colette was living at its centre. She was familiar with many leading personalities within the literary and theatrical worlds, and friends with many of them. She and Willy had been a modern couple, their lives led in the public gaze. Their portraits were painted by the leading society painters, cartoons were printed in the daily press and, even apart, they were to continue to provide more grist to the daily mill of gossip and scandal.

Willy had opened many doors for this young girl from the provinces and, as Sido had written in one of her many letters to her daughter, it was Willy who had revealed to Colette her talent as a writer. Their divorce would be very bitter, and each would take vengeance on the other in works published many years later.

Willy died in 1931, penniless and seemingly forgotten. However, he was accorded a last act of recognition by his Parisian friends, colleagues and public, when three thousand people followed his funeral procession to the Montparnasse Cemetery.

Colette was not among them.

Cover for Claudine à l'école, *with illustration by Emilio Della Sudda*

UN FRAN

UN FRANC

EXPOSITION UNIVERSELLE I8

TICKET D'ENTRÉE

n° 0,812,27

MASSIAS DEL.   G.RICH

SITION UNIVER

ET D'ENT

0,812

Chapter 4

Living alone — Le Domaine des Monts-Bouccons —

At the least prompting of my memory, I can see the dark roof tiles of Les Monts-Bouccons, its neo-classical Directoire façade—which I am sure really only dated from the reign of Charles X—the colour of a faded yellow cameo, its copses, its tree sculpted in rock in the style of Hubert Robert. The house, the little farm, the five or six hectares that surrounded them, Willy seemed to give them to me: 'All this is for you.' Three years later, he took them away: 'This is no longer yours, nor mine.'

In September 1901, following the success of *Claudine à l'école*, Willy bought a property in the Franche-Comté region east of Paris. The following year, he purchased the adjoining farm and for the first time since her marriage, Colette was able to enjoy the freedom and solitude of life in the country.

The Franche-Comté is a mountainous region bordering Switzerland to the east, its lush and fertile rural landscape flanked by the Vosges Mountains to the north and the Jura Mountains to the south. The capital, Besançon, is nestled into a loop of the River Doubs, protected by an impressive citadel built in the early eighteenth century by Vauban, one of France's greatest military engineers. The attractive city centre is of interest historically, with a number of fine stone buildings. It also has an important literary history, particularly as the cradle of French romanticism—Victor Hugo was born here, and there are links with other romantic writers, including Stendhal, Flaubert and Balzac.

Le Domaine des Monts-Bouccons, the property that Willy bought, still stands today, just a few kilometres from the centre of Besançon. It was a grey and misty day when we visited, with occasional showers. We had left Paris early that morning and were met at Besançon's train station by the charming gentleman who is responsible for the city's cultural heritage. I had been in contact with him by email and he had generously agreed to show me the house. He proved to be a wonderful guide, taking us not only to see Les Monts-Bouccons, but also guiding us around Besançon and its citadel. He provided an introduction to the city librarian, and was a wealth of information about the house and its history.

Les Monts-Bouccons had come to the attention of Willy through an old friend, Jules Bruneteau, a native of Besançon. Willy's family came from this part of France and he and Bruneteau had been officers in the reserve in Besançon. Willy was not to keep the property for long, however, and in 1907, when funds were short once again,

Le Domaine des Monts-Bouccons

he sold it back to his old friend. The house remained in the hands of the descendants of Bruneteau's daughter until it was recently bought by the city of Besançon.

The accretions of the years sit lightly on the fabric of the house at Les Monts-Bouccons, even if its façade is more faded than it was in Colette's time and the shutters are in need of a coat of paint. Some of the adjoining land has been sold off, but the house is still surrounded by a park with meadows and woods of fir trees, Lebanese cedars, weeping willows, chestnut and linden trees. A few of the orchard's old fruit trees remain standing, and a narrow path leads from the house to the glen where a rocky outcrop forms a secluded small amphitheatre. A spindly jasmine grows by the front door and the building is sheltered by a magnificent stand of trees.

As I walked along the little path to the secluded grove, I became aware of the intense perfume of a flowering bush—a *Syringa vulgaris*, I was told, a white lilac. Its perfume was not unlike that of the frangipani, whose fragrance wafts through the streets of Sydney in summer. Colette always believed that the sense of smell was the most subtle of our senses, revealing to us memories both of pleasure and tears.

From 1901 to 1905, Colette spent every summer and autumn at Les Monts-Bouccons. It was a small house, Colette wrote in a letter to one of her friends, 'rather old-fashioned, dark and damp', but the orchard trees produced plenty of fruit, and it fulfilled Colette's dream of a country retreat. She gardened, picked fruit, gathered mushrooms and enjoyed the rhythm of country life. She would rise at six o'clock in summer, seven in autumn, and be outside, 'enjoying the roses heavy with dew, the red leaves of the cherry trees trembling in the red glow of a November morning'.

She bought a little cart and harness, and would set off across the countryside, picking wild roses, mushrooms, herbs and wild strawberries. The empty seat next to her would be filled with flowers, apples, chestnuts and, on one excursion, some very fine wines of Burgundy, 'all fire and flame', aged bottles that she had bought at a ridiculously cheap price in a little country inn that was changing hands. 'Ah

yes,' said our guide, when I mentioned this. 'That little inn was called Au Bout du Monde and it used to belong to my grandparents.'

Colette wondered if her Parisian friends would recognise her, dressed as she was in 'an apron, a pink cotton sun-bonnet and dirty hob-nailed boots'. An article that appeared in the local newspaper in 1903 described Colette and her surroundings. The journalist had gone in search of Willy, but had been delighted with his encounter with a charming and playful 'shepherdess in the style of Watteau'. Colette was dressed in a brightly coloured floating dress, her saucy face framed by light brown hair, tousled, cut short and topped by a rustic panama hat. With a rake in her hand, she emerged from under a charming bower of foliage and greenery. 'Welcome,' she said, 'come inside and we can talk at ease.'

They went into the salon. It was furnished simply, with a couple of 'modern' chairs, a piano, a few tables, a bookshelf, some armchairs and a few knick-knacks. Paintings by local artists hung on the walls, interspersed with photographs and sketches. It all seemed a little bit haphazard and unpremeditated, the journalist wrote, and yet it gave an impression of harmony, liveliness and gaiety—a most appropriate environment for the totally unexpected personality of Madame Gauthier-Villars.

For the next couple of hours, Colette responded in a lively and amusing manner to the journalist's questions. Why were they in Besançon? Because of Willy's family connections to the town. They came every year for a few months, she added, and hoped that at some time they would take up permanent residence.

Colette then talked of Willy's literary output, including the *Claudine* series. In response to the journalist's questions, Colette admitted to having collaborated on the series. 'Yes, I admit it,' she said. 'I have denied it for a long time, as I would prefer that Willy be recognised as solely responsible, but he continues to insist on my contribution and so I must bow to his will.' Clearly, Colette was enjoying herself in this interview!

Colette loved to garden when she was at Les Monts-Bouccons, left in a field of poppies, above picking fruit in the orchard

She went on to talk about Polaire and her portrayal of Claudine in the theatre, and of the projects she and Willy were currently working on. As the interview drew to a close, the journalist was surprised to learn that she had been married for nine years. He had assumed his interviewee to be no more than twenty-two or twenty-three years old. Colette had clearly captivated this eager and impressionable journalist from the provinces, as she played the role of the ingénue wife.

The time Colette spent at Les Monts-Bouccons was productive. It was here that she wrote the last of the *Claudine* novels, *Claudine s'en va* (*Claudine and Annie*), along with *Minne* and *Les Égarements de Minne*, which were later published as a single novel, *L'Ingénue libertine*. Once again, all three of these novels were published under Willy's name. More importantly, it was also here at Les Monts-Bouccons that Colette wrote the first book that would be published in her own name, *Dialogues de bêtes*, with the dedication '*To amuse Willy*'.

For the first time, Colette gave herself the pleasure of writing about something other than love. In *Dialogues de bêtes*, she leaves behind the titillating, gossipy, Parisian world of the later *Claudine* novels, and creates a series of imagined conversations between her cat and dog, Kiki-la-Doucette and Toby-Chien, who always accompanied her to Les Monts-Bouccons. While there is a certain preciousness to these conversations between the two animals as they report and comment on what is going on between their mistress and master, 'the two-legged ones' as they call them, they expressed some of Colette's deeper feelings.

'I want to do what I want to do,' she wrote through the voice of Toby-Chien. Colette had had enough of all those young women who threw themselves at Willy, of his many affairs. She would abandon him to them—let him see them for what they really were. There would be no more first nights, no more exhibition openings—she was sick of seeing all those faces exhausted by the effort of resisting the signs of age. She no longer wanted to go on living a lie; she wanted to be true to herself, to live how she wanted to, to do what she wanted to do, to continue to cherish Willy—to give him her body that didn't like to be shared, her gentle heart and her freedom. She wanted to write 'sad and chaste books which speak only of landscapes, flowers, sorrow, pride, and the candour of charming beasts that are afraid of man'.

Dialogues de bêtes was published in 1904 under the name of Colette Willy, the name she would use until 1923; after this date, all her work was signed simply 'Colette'. The publication of her little book provided the opportunity for Colette to establish a correspondence with Francis Jammes, a poet whose work she greatly admired. She sent him a copy of *Dialogues de bêtes*, asking him for his opinion. A year later, when she was about to publish a new edition, enlarged with three more dialogues, she asked Jammes to write a preface, which he agreed to do. Jammes's appreciation of Colette's talent allowed him to see her as something other than the woman of the Parisian legend. He presented another image of Colette—no closer to reality than that of the Parisian libertine, but one that pleased Colette a great deal.

'Madame Colette Willy has never ceased to be a country housewife par excellence,' he wrote in his preface. 'Up at dawn, she gives hay to the horses, corn to the chickens, cabbages to the rabbits, grain to the canary, snails to the ducks, bran water to the pigs. At eight o'clock she prepares coffee for herself and the maid. Hardly a day goes past when she doesn't consult *The Countrywoman's Almanac*. Neither the apiary, nor the orchard, the vegetable garden nor the stable holds any secrets from Madame Colette Willy.'

This preface was the beginning of what Colette was to call her rehabilitation. She and Jammes maintained a warm correspondence until 1906, when a certain modesty prevented her from continuing to write to him. She thought that her performances as a mime artist made her no longer worthy of his friendship. 'Before some,' she wrote, 'the fact that I have performed as a faun at the Théâtre de Mathurins makes me arrogant; before you, it makes me humble.'

Francis Jammes led a life of solitude and retreat in the country; he acknowledged the difference in their lives, but saw no difference in their hearts. A few years later, in 1911, he asked Colette to write something for a magazine that was dedicating a special edition to his work. 'When I am old,' she wrote, 'I will go to see Francis Jammes … Then I will be bold enough to speak to him and to say: This is me, see me for who I am. I have never left, my whole life long, the gate all entwined with flowers, where you left me on the threshold of *Dialogues de bêtes* … I never cut my hair, I never toured from town to town, I never danced half-naked. Then Francis Jammes will smile, lighting up his face that I have never seen.'

While at Les Monts-Bouccons, Colette also wrote *La Retraite sentimentale* (*Retreat from Love*). Published under the name of Colette Willy, it is the story of Annie, a young woman who loved men too much, and Marcel, a man who didn't love women at all. It would be the last of the *Claudine* novels.

The novel takes place at Casamène, a property in the country, modelled on Les Mont-Bouccons, where Claudine has come to spend time with Annie while Renaud, her husband, is in a sanatorium.

Casamène is perched on the rounded shoulder of a little mountain covered in low oak trees, whose leaves have not yet been burnt by October's flames. Annie's place is an old one-storey house, warm in the winter and cool in the summer, a dwelling without airs, but not without grace. The little sculpted marble pediment ... is flaking off, quite yellow with mildew, and, under the five wobbly front-door steps, a toad sings in the evening, his amorous song full of pearls.

Casamène is a retreat for Annie and Claudine, just as Les Mont-Bouccons was Colette's safe haven. For Claudine, it is a retreat from her life as a couple, as Renaud slides towards death, and Casamène becomes the new focus of her attention. She takes possession of it, from the grapevines she tends to the imprisoned springs lying deep beneath the earth and that come to the surface tasting of sandstone and mildew. She finds sustenance in nature, as had the young Claudine, in the woods and springs of Montigny.

By 1907, when *La Retraite sentimentale* was published, Les Monts-Bouccons was about to be sold and Colette's marriage with Willy was over. She was living in her own little ground-floor apartment in the rue de Villejust and had begun to perform mime and dance. It was the beginning of a new way of life.

❧

Physical and mental discipline were an important part of Colette's regime at Les Monts-Bouccons. She was developing resources that had nothing to do with literature. She had installed exercise bars in the garden, as she had in the apartment on rue de Courcelles. On trapezes and parallel bars, she practised 'the timid balancing tricks of a woman who is afraid of breaking something or of being beaten by her husband'. Before their separation, Willy visited from time to time, but only for a few brief days. Colette still seemed to be holding on to her dream of life as a couple in the countryside, but Willy's departures wounded her. As she grew accustomed to her solitude, however, she felt herself become stronger.

Colette's separation from Willy in 1906 left her with no financial resources. She had no access to any of the income from the *Claudine* books, and never had any money of her own. The only book that had appeared in her name at that time was *Dialogues de bêtes*, so how could she possibly earn an income from writing? She had no career. And so her thoughts turned to the theatre. 'The music hall,' she wrote, 'is the career of those who have no career.'

Colette had always been interested in the theatre, and she would continue to be throughout her life. For a number of years she had been taking mime classes with Georges Wague, a highly respected performer who contributed to restoring the reputation of mime in the early years of the twentieth century.

Colette's appearance on the stage was considered by many to be scandalous. It may have been acceptable for her to perform in private, but a public performance was a different matter, particularly given the rather risqué nature of some of the mimes in which she performed. Sido was one of her harshest critics, believing that the theatre was diverting her daughter from her true vocation as a writer.

Like Willy, Colette understood the popular appeal of the theatre. She had experienced it first-hand through the stage adaptation of the *Claudine* novels, and through her husband she had met many people who worked in the theatre—writers, directors and performers. Her friend Marguerite Moreno was an actor with La Comédie-Française and with Sarah Bernhardt's theatre. By embracing the theatre, Colette was claiming her freedom to be the person she wanted to be, to do the things she wanted to do.

Over the next seven years, Colette performed in both Paris and the provinces. She performed as a mime artist in a number of new pieces with Georges Wague and his wife, and also acted in plays, including playing the role of Claudine originally created by Polaire.

Colette's performances met with varied critical responses, but few critics were insensitive to her charms. One critic wrote a glowing review of her qualities as a performer, likening them to her writing—spontaneous and incisive. Another compared her to the famous dancers of the time, Loie Fuller and Isadora Duncan. What he saw was new, original and almost poignant. Another critic wrote that her movements had the intelligence of animals, plants and children who gave free rein to their instincts.

Others were less complimentary, however, saying that she did not know how to move on stage, let alone how to dance. Colette didn't take these criticisms to heart. She enjoyed the work she was doing in the theatre. It was earning her an income and she took pride in her body, writing at this time that it was through her body that she thought, and that it was more intelligent than her brain. The many photos of Colette from this period of her life show an extremely expressive face and a curvaceous and supple body.

Even as she pursued the demanding routine of touring and performing, Colette continued to write, publishing *Les Vrilles de la vigne* (*Tendrils of the Vine*) in 1908 and *La Vagabonde* (*The Vagabond*) in 1910. In *La Vagabonde*, she drew on her personal experiences, recounting the quest for independence of a recently divorced woman, Renée, who turns to performance as a way to escape the confines of her earlier life. The lover who wants to share her life is rejected, and the friendly camaraderie of her colleagues provides an antidote to melancholy. Unfettered and free, Renée knows that physical pleasure is not enough. It will always be a hunger in her life, but she will not allow herself to be entrapped by it. In Renée, Colette had created her second literary alter ego. The character was to reappear a couple of years later in the book's sequel, *L'Entrave* (*The Captive*).

Colette and Willy were finally divorced in 1910. It had been a bitter time, with charge and counter-charge from each side. The last straw for Colette was when she discovered that Willy had sold the rights to the *Claudine* novels to the publishers. Although she had lost all financial rights, she obtained recognition as co-author, and from 1910 until after the Second World War, all editions of the *Claudine* novels carried the names of both Willy and Colette Willy as authors.

❧

The demanding life of rehearsals, touring and performing was very different from Colette's secluded country life at Les Monts-Bouccons. It had been a short-lived interlude, but one that had given Colette the resources she had needed to begin her life anew. She returned to Besançon from time to time when she was touring, and stayed at the Hotel de Paris in the centre of town. The Brasserie du Commerce, where she would enjoy the local cuisine, still stands next door.

After our visit to Les Monts-Bouccons, my partner and I were happy to take the advice of our informed guide and stop for lunch there. It is a fine old brasserie, the only survivor of seventy fine cafes that existed in Besançon at the time of the Belle

With Toby-Chien

Époque. It was opened in 1873, the year of Colette's birth, and still retains its elegant décor with sculpted stuccowork and globe-shaped lights reflected in the tall mirrors.

Colette was a familiar sight in the town and she had dealings with the local businesses. Some of the letters amongst the small collection held in the Besançon library are from Colette to the local pharmacist, asking him to provide a treatment for Willy's liver. Her letters were addressed in Colette's inimitable, witty style—to Monsieur Duchaillut, 'pharmacist of the first rank', on one envelope and 'generous gentleman and the honour of French pharmacy' on another.

As Les Monts-Bouccons receded in Colette's memory, it joined her childhood home in Saint-Sauveur, taking on the dimensions of a lost paradise.

> *We hold on, by an image, to vanished possessions, but it is the separation that creates the image, that ties together the bouquet. What would I have remembered of Les Monts-Bouccons if Willy had not taken the property from me? Perhaps less than I remember today. Like with all loves lost at the time of its flowering, I asked, 'Will I be able to live without Les Monts-Bouccons?' And then, I attached first of all to my bosom and then to my wall, the bouquet of yellow leaves, mixed with cherries half preserved by the fierce summers of Franche-Comté, bunches of sleepy wasps, taken at dawn in basketfuls, from their strong underground nests; a plume of spotted feathers, the quill-feathers of my five goshawks, hunters of snakes and lizards, perched insolently on the little quince-tree. They would hold my eye as I approached and then fly off, spreading in the air a vast wheel of wings … This is my memory of Les Monts-Bouccons.*

Illustration by André Dignimont for La Retraite sentimentale

Chapter 5
— Brittany — the vagabond years —

Windmills turn in the distance. In the little stations that the train passes through, Breton caps, the first white Breton caps, are flowering like daisies … I am dazzled as I enter this yellow kingdom of broom and gorse. Gold, copper, bronze too—for pale rape-seed is part of the mix—make these barren heathlands glow with an unbearable light. I lean my cheek and my open hands against the windowpane of the carriage and am surprised not to find it warm. We are passing through fire, mile after mile of gorse in bloom, a desolate richness that discourages even the goats, where butterflies, weighed down by the warm perfume of pepper and half-ripened peaches, twirl with torn wings.

The Breton caps no longer flower like daisies, but there are remnants of barren heathland that glow with the yellow and pink of broom and gorse. The little fishing village of Cancale clings to the steep cliffs, from where the narrow path of the *sentier des douaniers* (the customs officers' track) winds its way along the cliff tops, descending steeply into the little bays between Cancale and Saint-Malo. In one of these little bays, the house called Rozven stands, its solemn façade and silent presence disturbed only by the sound of the lapping waves.

This house was for many years filled with the sounds of laughter and talk as Colette gathered friends and family around her, delighting in the sea and sand, in the bounteousness of the ocean and the ever-changing light.

The house came to Colette through Missy, the Marquise de Belbeuf, whom she first met in 1905. With Willy, Colette had regularly spent evenings at Le Cercle des arts et de la mode on avenue Victor-Hugo—a club frequented by the literary and artistic world, including luminaries of the Parisian lesbian set. It was here that Colette and the marquise met, much to the amusement of Willy, who did not move from the baccarat table. He had never been inclined to discourage his wife from pursuing lesbian liaisons. Indeed, he seemed amused by them.

Colette and Missy soon became a couple, but this liaison was different, and was not just a passing affair. Missy would be Colette's partner for a number of years. Ten years older than Colette, she was a familiar figure in Parisian lesbian circles. Mathilde (her given name) was the daughter of the Duc de Morny, a highly successful, although somewhat corrupt, businessman and statesman during the period of the Second Empire. Her mother was a Russian princess who was incapable of loving her children, and Missy's childhood had been unhappy and lonely. She was married off at the age of eighteen to the Marquis de Belbeuf, from whom she separated four years later. With a substantial personal fortune, Missy was now able to live as she pleased, so she dressed as a man, in elegant, finely tailored clothes. She wore her hair cut very short, smoked cigars and preferred to be called Max or Uncle Max. Missy was ostracised by many in Parisian society, as it was not permitted for women to dress as men, and none of the other high-profile lesbians of the time ever did so.

The relationship between Colette and Missy was of course the source of much gossip, and the Parisian press delighted in keeping its readers up to date with the latest exploits of both Willy and his new paramour, Meg Villars, and of Colette and the Marquise de Belbeuf. Colette was going through the protracted process of separation and divorce from Willy at this time, and was launching her career as a performer. After her separation, Colette's apartment in the rue de Villejust was just around the corner from Missy's home on rue Georges-Ville, where she was often to be found.

Gossip was to turn to scandal in 1906, however, when Missy and Colette appeared in a mime performance together at the Moulin Rouge. Missy had also been taking

mime lessons with Georges Wague, and had written the scenario for a pantomime entitled *Dream of Egypt*, in which an Egyptologist is seduced by a mummy who comes to life, the scene culminating in a long kiss. A brouhaha had been building in the lead-up to the performance, with Colette defending Missy's right to perform on the stage. Why should the fact that a woman belongs to French aristocracy prevent her from doing what she wants, Colette asked in a letter to one of the offending newspapers. The Moulin Rouge added further spice by printing the coats of arms of the Morny and Belbeuf families on the publicity poster, without Missy's permission, and her stage name of Yssim fooled no one.

On the night of the performance, the Moulin Rouge was packed, including a large claque of members of the conservative aristocratic Jockey Club, who booed and hissed. Willy was in attendance and was caught up in the mêlée when he tried to lead the applause. He was forced to leave the theatre. The police took out an order preventing Missy from performing, and the following night her part was played by Georges Wague and the pantomime was renamed *Dream of the Orient*. The scandal continued and a second police order prevented the show from continuing.

The repercussions for Colette from this scandal were insignificant compared with the fallout for Willy and Missy; Colette had already put her reputation at risk by appearing on the stage. Willy was shown the door at *L'Echo de Paris*, where he regularly published articles, causing him serious financial difficulties. Missy's public reputation was permanently tarnished.

❧

For the next few years, when Colette wasn't touring in her various theatrical productions, she lived with Missy at rue Torricelli, near the place des Ternes. For the first time since leaving Saint-Sauveur, Colette had found someone who really cared for her and protected her.

Missy and Colette in Dream of Egypt

Colette as a faun in Le Désir, l'amour et le chimère

Missy had renovated the upper level of this new home at rue Torricelli for herself and the lower for Colette. She often went on tour with Colette, looking after her and tending to her smallest needs. Touring as a music-hall artist was not easy—cold theatres, squalid hotels, early starts to catch the train to the next town. Colette was noting it all down and would later draw on these notes for her book *L'Envers du music-hall* (*Backstage at the Music-Hall*), published in 1913. Far from being the front-of-house view of the theatre, with its lights and make-up, glitter and smiles, this was the sweat and exhaustion of the backstage, the yellow skin that never saw the light of day, the miserable existence eked out by young girls who were born in the streets, the stories of illicit abortions, of exploitative lovers. Colette had seen it all at close quarters.

There was respite from this life when Missy travelled with her. They stayed in comfortable hotels, travelled first class, dined in better restaurants. Colette became increasingly dependent on the little luxuries of life that Missy could offer her. She also grew to rely on her to ward off her feelings of loneliness. Missy was in many ways a substitute mother for Colette; her maternal tenderness and

love permitted Colette to continue to be the child. She had looked for a father figure in Willy, and found him wanting. Now she was looking for a mother figure in Missy—an indulgent mother figure who did not make demands as her real mother did.

Sido did not see a rival in Missy. She was no prude, and had no argument about her daughter's relationship with a woman. Indeed she welcomed this new relationship, knowing that Missy was looking after her daughter, bringing her material and emotional comfort. For her part, Missy had no expectations of Colette. She recognised her for the spoilt, self-indulgent creature that she was, and was happy to do all she could to keep her in her presence, including indulging her affair with Auguste Hériot, heir to the Grands Magasins du Louvre department-store fortune. She also helped Colette deal with her distress and unhappiness at the definitive split with Willy. Colette's feelings towards Willy were always complex—right to the end, she harboured thoughts that they might become a couple once again.

For a number of years, Missy and Colette continued to holiday at Le Crotoy. In 1910, they decided to look for a house to buy in Brittany, where the climate was milder. It was Missy who found Rozven—'rose of the winds'—on the coast between Cancale and Saint-Malo, but although it was she who was buying the house, the owner refused to sell to a woman who dressed as a man, and so Colette signed the contract of purchase. While Colette continued her theatrical tours, Missy supervised the renovations and furnished the house.

Missy was to enjoy Rozven for only a short time, for Colette's life was about to change yet again. At the end of 1910, she began writing a regular column for the daily newspaper *Le Matin*. Within a few months, she was in a new relationship with Henry de Jouvenel, one of the newspaper's co-editors.

Missy was devastated by this betrayal. For five years, she had been a constant, loving and generous companion to Colette, supporting her through the difficult times of her divorce with Willy and the legal battle over the rights to her works. Colette's affair with Auguste Hériot had not been a serious threat, as Colette had found him a charming but weak companion. In Jouvenel, however, she had met someone who was her intellectual equal, ambitious and complex, and a passionate lover. She had seen the glimmer of happiness that life with a man she loved and admired offered. She was not going to let that escape her.

In August 1911, Missy wrote to Georges Wague informing him that she and Colette had separated. There was no longer room in Colette's life for Missy, but Colette insisted on keeping Rozven. She was not going to lose yet another house that had become a special retreat. Her signature was on the contract of purchase and she believed Missy could easily afford to let her keep the house. She even argued with Missy over her right to keep her own furniture. Sadly, Colette had become used to being indulged by Missy. Sido had been right when she had written to her daughter three years earlier that she was so lucky to have found such a tender loving friend. 'You are so used to being spoiled that I cannot imagine what would happen if you weren't.'

Missy reluctantly relinquished Rozven, buying herself a villa nearby. For Missy,

who had been so generous towards Colette, it had been a bitter parting.

Colette and Missy renewed contact twenty years later, and their letters reveal a sincere friendship. However, this too would be troubled when Colette published what was clearly a portrait of Missy in her book *Ces plaisirs* (later republished as *Le Pur et l'impur* (*The Pure and the Impure*). As the years went by, Missy lived an increasingly isolated and lonely life. By the time of her death in 1944, she had given away her entire fortune and was living in poverty. If not for the generosity of the playwright Sacha Guitry, who paid her account at a little restaurant in her neighbourhood, she would have gone hungry in the last years of her life.

This was the woman about whom Colette had written that she 'could not imagine her life without her, without her sweetness, her smile that was more sad than gay'. From the beginning, Colette had been aware of Missy's melancholy, the melancholy of those people of ambiguous sexuality for whom happiness was always elusive.

℘

Missy's legacy was Rozven. From 1911 until 1926, Colette presided over her bucolic summer retreat, surrounded initially by friends and then by her new family. She loved this 'burnt and fragrant coast' with its 'necklace of lighthouses that glows around the bays in the evening'. She learnt to swim, to fish for shrimp, to catch crabs, to indulge in what she called a 'marine intoxication'.

The house itself was large and solid, built in the grey stone typical of the region. It looked out over a grassy slope leading down to the beach. Even after Missy's renovations, it was never anything more than a house of rudimentary comfort, but one that welcomed many people. There was a copious kitchen garden and orchard, and the catch of the day provided an abundance of seafood for meals.

Colette's letters record her delight. Mornings were spent on the secluded beach or exploring the cliffs and headlands. The tide was a bearer of treasures—of mauve coral and polished shells, and sometimes casks of whale oil from a distant wreck. At lunchtime, everyone gathered back at the house, where they indulged in a fine feast of local produce—crabs, crayfish, lobsters and prawns—finishing the meal with one of the local Breton cakes, such as the *kouign-amann*, a rich bread-and-butter pudding, which I tasted for the first time at one of the little restaurants in Cancale and found very delicious.

There is still a fish market at Cancale, a centre for oyster production on the western edge of the wide shallow Bay of Mont Saint-Michel. From our room in a little hotel on the cliff top at Cancale we could see the fortified abbey of Mont Saint-Michel in the distance. The tides along this coast are huge, leaving vast expanses of sand as the sea goes out, boats left perched on the sand waiting for the return of the tide. Oysters, lobsters, mussels, prawns and abalone form the basis of the fishing industry here and of the regional gastronomy, along with the famous *crêpes* and *galettes*. Until the collapse of the industry due to overfishing, this area was the centre of cod fishing. The boats would set off for Newfoundland from Saint-Malo and other ports, returning six months later.

It is impossible to escape the seafaring traditions of this part of Brittany. The rugged coastline faces north to the English Channel, with steep rocky cliffs that give way to sheltered beaches where the grassy fields meet the sand dunes. On the cliff tops, windswept heathlands with yellow gorse and clumps of bent and gnarled trees provide dramatic views of the offshore islands, the waves beating against the rocks below, the coast's distant points marked by their lonely lighthouses. As we walked around the headland on a blustering day, I appreciated the unchanging nature of this coastline. It is still a remote and wild landscape.

With the exception of the war years, Colette spent her summers at Rozven. She was often accompanied by friends—other writers, the playwright Léopold Marchand, with whom she collaborated on the adaptation for the theatre of a number of her novels, and the poet Hélène Picard, who became her secretary at *Le Matin* in 1920.

Colette and Henry de Jouvenel were married in 1912. Jouvenel would visit Rozven from time to time, but he was often kept away by his work. Bertrand and Renaud, his sons from previous relationships, would frequently be entrusted to Colette's care

*Holiday snapshots at Rozven with family and friends –
her daughter and stepson on the left*

in Rozven, where they joined their much younger half-sister Bel-Gazou, who was born in 1913. Colette wrote to Marguerite Moreno that she was 'lazy and living only in her body, surrounded by a horde of terrors. These Jouvenel brothers, let loose, play with the dogs, roll around on the ground, shout and leap about'.

It was in the indolent atmosphere of Rozven that Colette began an affair with her 17-year-old stepson, Bertrand de Jouvenel. The affair began in 1920, when Colette was almost fifty, and was to last for five years. Colette was still a powerfully seductive woman, and Henry de Jouvenel's attentions had for some time been focused elsewhere. There was clearly a very strong attraction between Colette and Bertrand; she provided him with love and tenderness, and with the discipline and direction that had not been forthcoming from his parents. Colette was full of energy and passion that she was happy to bestow on this young man, following her own advice to her dear friend Marguerite Moreno: 'take advantage of a temptation that passes and indulge it. What can we be sure of, other than what we hold in our arms, at the very moment when we are holding it. The opportunity to possess is rare.'

The Rozven years were extremely fruitful for Colette. She had published *La Vagabonde* in 1910, *L'Entrave* (*The Captive*) and *L'Envers du music-hall* in 1913. Three collections of stories and articles were published during the war, followed by *Mitsou* in 1919 and her great masterpieces, *Chéri* in 1920 and *La Maison de Claudine* (*My Mother's House*) in 1922.

More than any other book she had written, *Chéri* brought Colette's work to the attention of her peers. The novel is set in 1910, as the Belle Époque is drawing to a close. Léa is a courtesan, in her late forties; she is ageing gracefully and maintaining rigorous control of her looks and her relationships. She is the mistress of Chéri, the spoilt 25-year-old son of another courtesan. He has been brought up to be idle, to have no purpose in life other than pleasure. Léa envelops Chéri with a maternal and voluptuous love, but Chéri is to be married off and the relationship between them must change. Léa leaves Paris and Chéri is devastated by jealousy and loss. The scene of their reunion when she returns to Paris is masterly. Léa loses the control that has defined her relationship with Chéri, and in doing so, loses Chéri.

Chéri is a novel about the power play between lovers. At the end of the book, it is Chéri who holds the reins of power. At the end of the sequel, *La Fin de Chéri* (*The Last of Chéri*), published six years later, Léa has regained control. The sequel describes the tragic end of this love story, when Chéri returns from the war to find himself even more disconnected from his family and friends. His wife and mother-in-law, his own mother and his friends are all preoccupied. There has been a revolution in sexual mores; business is taking centre stage and social hierarchies are shifting. The war has changed many things and Chéri cannot see a role for himself in this new world. Léa, too, has changed. She has become an old woman; all Chéri can recognise in this shapeless form is her voice. Léa will survive; Chéri will not. At the end of the novel, he shoots himself. Chéri's death is the death of an era.

Chéri is not the story of Colette's relationship with her stepson Bertrand. When they first became lovers, *Chéri* was already being serialised in *La Vie Parisienne*. The novel grew out of a series of stories Colette had written for *Le Matin* before the war, in which the character was originally called Clouk. He was a sad, rather pathetic young man, possibly inspired by the wealthy heir Auguste Hériot.

Léa is not Colette. Nonetheless, there are aspects of Léa's character that have much in common with Colette. She shares her love of good food, her down-to-earth practicality, as well as her passion. Colette would live this relationship, but not until she had created it as literature.

When I re-read these books, after having seen the recent film based on them, I was struck once again by Colette's masterly depiction of her characters, the sureness of the dialogue, the pared-back refinement of her prose. Through these works, Colette was redefining herself as a writer, developing an intensely personal style that was both energetic and spare, and that increasingly earned her the praise of other writers.

Colette, her husband Henri de Jouvenel and stepson Bertrand

Rozven and her relationship with Bertrand de Jouvenel did, however, provide the inspiration for Colette's next novel, *Le Blé en herbe* (*The Ripening Seed*), in which her descriptions of the Breton landscape are the setting for the seduction of a young man by an older woman and the awakening of adolescent love. The story of two teenagers, Phil and Vinca, and the lady in white is set in the landscape that surrounds Rozven, where at high tide the sea comes right up to the sandy meadow in front of the house and where, as the summer drew to a close, the families would have 'dinner by lamplight, the doors opened onto a green sunset where a spindle of pink copper still floated' and 'you could hear the listless, even ebbing of the neap tide'.

The Ripening Seed is Colette's hymn to Brittany. The novel is steeped in the colours and perfumes with which she was so familiar. 'Brittany bathed me in a milky blue,' she wrote many years later, 'an airy blue that, at dawn, hung from the branches of

the apple tree, the masts of the boats and the jagged rocks'. The character Vinca was infused with this same blue, from the colour of her eyes, the 'colour of a spring shower of rain', to her woollen beret, the same light blue as the dune thistles.

The novel is also Colette's homage to adolescent love and the seductive attraction between an older woman and a younger man. I remember being unable to put this novel down when first I read it. I was in my teens and was captivated by the mix of the familiar and the unfamiliar, the seaside holidays, the emotional turmoil of young love, the sense of being on the verge of a new beginning. In an interview, Colette described the genesis of the novel:

> For a long time I had wanted to write a one-act play for the theatre ... The curtain goes up, the stage is in darkness, two invisible characters are talking about love with a great deal of knowledge and experience. At the end, the lights go up and the surprised audience sees that the characters are fifteen and sixteen years old. I wanted to show that passionate love knows no age and that love only has one language ... I said nothing more in The Ripening Seed. All I did was to insert into the story a few landscapes from around Cancale which had made a strong impression on me.

Colette completed the novel in 1923. 'I have finished,' she wrote to Marguerite Moreno, 'not without torment.' The manuscript's last page had taken her a day to write—twenty lines, she said, where she struggled to get the right sense of proportion, where the fragility of young love was balanced by the resilience of youth.

Like many of her novels, *The Ripening Seed* was serialised, appearing in *Le Matin* from July 1922. The account of the seduction of the young man by an older woman was already testing the readers of *Le Matin*, but the depiction of a sexual relationship between two young people before marriage was too much for the bourgeois morality of the time, and in March 1923 the newspaper's management refused to publish any further episodes. When the novel was published in its entirety by Flammarion in July 1923, it met with critical success and caused something of a furore. 'An admirable book,' wrote one critic, 'stripped bare ... depicting adolescence in all its fears and emotions, its overwhelming discoveries and its frail resources, its horizons at once so broad and yet so limited.'

The Ripening Seed was the first novel that Colette signed simply 'Colette'. In 1923, she was fifty years old. She had achieved an unassailable reputation as a writer, and needed to claim this status in her own name—not Colette Willy, nor Colette de

Jouvenel, but simply Colette. Legally, as a writer and as an individual, she now had only one name, her own. 'It has only taken thirty years of my life to get back to this point,' she wrote.

Meanwhile, her second marriage was coming towards an end. And while her liaison with her stepson Bertrand would last a few more years, and was emotionally significant for both of them, it too had no future. Bertrand's career, like that of his father, was to be in politics, and a relationship with his stepmother, who was more than twice his age, would not be to his advantage. It was time for them to give up their shared holidays in places like Gstaad and Algeria—and for Bertrand, like Chéri before him, to marry.

Summers at Rozven were a welcome break for Colette from the demands of her life as a journalist and literary editor at *Le Matin* in Paris. But even here, she continued to work. After mornings spent on the beach or walking along the cliff tops, she would retreat to her room to work.

As I stood on the terrace at Rozven, looking out over this private world of sea and sand, I was struck by how little it has changed since Colette's time here. The house has not been encroached upon in any way. It still sits sentinel over the beach and little bay, without another house in sight. A solitary couple were walking along the beach and I overheard them talking about the fact that the house had once belonged to Colette.

I had contacted the current owner, who unfortunately was not able to meet us at Rozven. Feel free to walk up to the house from the beach, he had said. As we were walking down the track to the house, I noticed that the gate was open and we could see that the gardener was at work tending the rose bushes. We walked down the drive and introduced ourselves. He welcomed us and invited us to wander in the garden at our will.

The grey stone of the building was covered with an autumn-tinted vine. From the front terrace, a little gate through a stone wall led to the protected back garden with its roses and flowers. Was this where Colette had her kitchen garden? I imagined so. The closed shutters of the house called out for children and laughter, for the presence of Colette and her entourage of friends. 'Don't forget your sandshoes,' she would write to friends about to visit from Paris, 'the sand and rocks are hot.'

It is easy to understand the attraction this Breton coast held for Colette. The expanse of the bays, the rapid rise of the tides, the grey-green colour of the sea under a cloudy sky, the wind whipping up the spray—they are all as Colette described them.

Later that day, we stood on the sea ramparts at Saint-Malo in the gusty wind, looking out on the watery landscape, reflecting on the centuries of seafaring that had been the heart and soul of the town. Colette had always been fascinated by the accounts of adventurers—of distant lands, exotic plants and animals—and a globe was never far from her reach.

It is a landscape to inspire dreams, a landscape that never lost its fascination for Colette. She recalled it nostalgically in her novella *Bella-Vista*, published in 1937.

The sulphurous smell of seaweed, a few broken shells, the wave which rose and fell without any strength, suddenly made me long for Brittany, for her tides, the big waves of Saint-Malo, which rolled in from afar and held captive, in their green-tinged swell, constellations of jellyfish and five-pointed starfish, and hermit crabs, tossed up by the waves. I longed for the rapid rise of the tide, plumed with spray, which refreshes the mussels, expiring as they wait, and the small oyster beds, and opens up the tentacles of the sea anemones and sea slugs.

The life of a performer

CASTEL-NOVEL-VARETZ-CORRÈZE
Phot. 1901

Carte d'Identité Professionnelle
des Journalistes
(LOI DU 29 MARS 1935)
DÉCRET DU 17 JANVIER 1936

Valable
- 1er AVR.
1939
- 1er AVR.
1940

4255 Mme COLETTE Sidonie (Goudeket M.)
PARIS-SOIR-
9 rue de Beaujolais-PARIS-
28-1-1873- St. Sauveur en Puisaye-

est JOURNALISTE professionnel
dans les conditions déterminées par la loi.

Pour la Commission
instituée par le Décret du 17 Janvier 1936
et pour certification de sa décision

LES PRIX DÉCOUTS A LA SIGNATURE

TIMBRE DE DIMENSION

SIGNATURE
DU TITULAIRE

N° DE LA CARTE
3543

Chapter 6

Madame la Baronne — Castel-Novel,
journalism and motherhood

You haven't seen Castel-Novel in springtime … The walls sparkle with lizards and turn golden with bees. … In summer a 300-year-old rosebush is like snow on the façade of the castle.

The family home of Henry de Jouvenel was Castel-Novel at Varetz in the Limousin, in south-west France. Henry grew up here before going to Paris. His father, Baron Raoul de Jouvenel, was a right-wing, anti-Semitic departmental representative in the Third Republic. Hot-tempered and ambitious, Henry opposed his father politically, supporting Dreyfus, marrying Claire Boas, the daughter of a wealthy Jewish industrialist, and working as a journalist with the then leftist paper *Le Matin*.

Jouvenel was also a philanderer, and four years after marrying Claire Boas, he left her and their son, Bertrand, to move in with his mistress, Isabelle de Comminges, who gave birth to Jouvenel's second son, Renaud, in 1907.

Many years later, Renaud described his father as 'an aristocrat although little infatuated by nobility, and a radical socialist of the old school—that is, sincerely democratic'. Of his relationship with Colette, he wrote that his father 'was of such a different class that I could not see what pleased him, putting aside the aesthetic taste of the period, in this literary debutante, who was known by everyone to have been one of those semi-naked dancers … he was throwing himself into the arms of a young odalisque, especially intelligent, lively, exciting, who knew how to love without being demanding and exhibited in many different ways a very original nature, even if she did seem somewhat immoderate'.

The attraction for Colette was easy to understand. Henry de Jouvenel was a man of substance, strong-willed and ambitious. He had a title, but not wealth, and was co-editor-in-chief at *Le Matin*. He was charming, handsome and, as Colette described in a letter to her friend Leon Hamel, 'tender, jealous, unsociable and incorrigibly honest'.

The beginning of their relationship was tumultuous. Isabelle de Comminges was furious when she learnt she had been supplanted, and she threatened to shoot Colette. Jouvenel's co-editor at *Le Matin* spirited Colette off to Rozven until things settled down, and Madame de Comminges consoled herself with a sea voyage with one of Colette's jilted lovers, the department-store heir Auguste Hériot.

This was a busy period for Colette. She was performing *La Chair* (*Flesh*) in Paris, as well as in Geneva and Lausanne, and was appearing in a new mime drama, *L'Oiseau de nuit* (*The Night Bird*), at the Gaîté-Rochechouart in Montparnasse. She

was producing a story a week for *Le Matin* and was soon to be a regular reporter for the paper, covering crime trials, hot-air balloon flights, visits by royalty and aviation club awards. In the midst of all this activity, she set off in July 1911 to visit Castel-Novel, Jouvenel's castle in the Corrèze.

> *As night fell, the towers were black against a cloudless sky, the ground floor was lit up with candles and paraffin lamps, highly polished silver, a large valet in a whitish livery, the big rosebush that had been left to grow wild—all was dark, crumbling, ravishing.*

The castle dates back to feudal times, and has been added to and altered over the centuries. Purchased in 1844 by the Jouvenel family, who came originally from nearby Aubazine, it stands on the top of a steep hill. Its solid circular tower built from rough-hewn stone probably dates back to the Middle Ages, while other more Italianate features are evidence of nineteenth-century renovations.

Castel-Novel is now a very fine hotel, and we decided to stay there for a couple of days. The castle remained in the Jouvenel family until 1956, when it was bought at auction by Raymond Parveaux, a baker in nearby Brive. Parveaux had always

Colette, her daughter Bel-Gazou and Gamelle, on the steps at Castel-Novel

harboured a dream of buying the property and turning it into a hotel and restaurant. His granddaughter told me that he had bought it without consulting his wife, who didn't necessarily share his dream. After many years of hard work, when a marquee was often installed on the lawns to host weddings and other celebrations to help pay for the significant investment the property required, Parveaux's dream was realised and Castel-Novel opened as a hotel in the Relais et Châteaux luxury accommodation chain. The property passed from Raymond Parveaux to his son, and is now in the hands of a member of the third generation, Sophie, who with her husband, Nicolas Soulié, in charge of the kitchens, manages it with finesse and discretion.

We had taken the train from Paris to Brive, where we hired a car to drive the short distance to Castel-Novel. The last few minutes of the drive took us along a narrow road that wound up through the trees to emerge at the top of a hill looking out over a wide valley, with the castle behind us. The castle's function had clearly altered since Colette's time, but its basic structure remained the same. The 300-year-old rose bush, whose abundance of white roses 'traced the milky-way' on the front of the castle at night, had been replaced by a vine with exuberant green foliage, which was just beginning to turn russet red when we visited in early autumn, covering the pink and cream stone of the façade and the old tower.

Inside, many of the original features remained—the circular stone staircase, the imposing stone fireplace in the dining room with its coat of arms, the grey and green monkey tapestries depicting the fables of La Fontaine adorning the ground-floor room used by Henry de Jouvenel. From what had been Colette's bedroom, on the second floor, there was a splendid view out over the treetops to the expanse of the valley beyond. Terraced gardens descended in front of the castle and, at the back, the steep hill was covered with tall birches, white poplars and fir trees, through which a dappled light reached the forest floor, already covered with fallen leaves. The memory of Colette was acknowledged subtly by the hotel—in the special menus which bore the names of Bel-Gazou and Colette.

After her first visit to Castel-Novel in 1911, Colette returned the following year, this time surrounded by Henry's family—his mother, his brother, Robert, and Edith, his half-sister. Colette found Castel-Novel to be 'worthy of the countryside that surrounds it'. Everyone was active—Henry on the farm, his mother playing tennis, Colette writing.

In December 1912, just a few months after the death of Sido, Colette and Jouvenel were married. Colette was pregnant, and in July of the following year she gave birth

Bel-Gazou, 'fruit of the Limousin earth',
as Colette called her, loved to visit the
farmyard where she would feed the hens,
calling them to her with her 'pétits, pétits,
pétits, eh, les povres pétits ...'

to a daughter. She was named Colette de Jouvenel, and was known as Bel-Gazou, the name Colette's father had given her when she was a girl. *Gazou* comes from *gazouiller*, meaning to chirp or twitter like a bird.

This late motherhood surprised Colette as much as it surprised others. Many years later, she wrote: 'This late child—I was forty years old—I remember accepting the certainty of its presence with a deep mistrust, not saying anything about it.' This reaction earned her a rebuke from one of her friends, who reprimanded: 'Do you know what you are doing? You are having the pregnancy of a man. A pregnancy should be more joyful. Put your hat on and come and have a strawberry ice cream with me at Poirée-Blanche.' Colette's pregnancy was running neck and neck with the need to finish her novel, *L'Entrave* (*The Captive*), but in the end the baby won and she put her pen aside.

As I sat on the terrace at Castel-Novel, sipping a glass of Pommery, Colette's preferred champagne, watching the sky turn a burnished red that was slowly absorbed by the blue-black of the night, sensing rather than seeing the shadowy swoop of the bats, my thoughts turned to Colette's daughter, who spent the first few years of her life here at Castel-Novel.

For Colette, Castel-Novel was always Bel-Gazou's country. War broke out the year after she was born, and the baby was left at Castel-Novel in the care of her English nurse. Colette and Jouvenel visited from time to time, but the demands of their work and the war meant that the time they spent at Castel-Novel was limited. For a young child, left alone for long periods of time with her governess and the few remaining staff, this must have been a lonely childhood. Castel-Novel was hardly comfortable at the time; there was no heating other than that provided by the fireplaces, and the rooms were vast and draughty.

When Colette did visit, she took great delight and pride in her daughter. Just a few months after her birth, she described her as 'a ruddy little Sidi [Colette's nickname for Henry], bossy, with a strong little body … a charming personality, with sudden outbursts of anger, which give way immediately, melting into smiles'.

By late spring of the following year, 1914, Bel-Gazou was an 'orchard, ruby-red like a fruit … a lily, tinted with the colours of dawn … a radiant little heifer, whose every feature was that of Sidi'. The metaphors tumbled after each other.

Her letters also described Colette's delight in Castel-Novel. The wild orchids are almost a metre high, she wrote, 'dark purple, luxurious flowers, and in the fields there are roses and flowering medlar apple trees … And the nightingales give themselves no time to drink or eat, since they sing from four in the afternoon to seven in the morning and from four in the morning to four in the afternoon.'

Colette was right to have mistrusted her pregnancy. There was too much else going on in her life for her to give a child the attention and love it needed. She admired her daughter, was in awe before the perfection of this little being, but she was never capable of enveloping her in maternal love. Many years later, Colette wrote that it wasn't until her daughter started to become a little girl, when she started to talk and to express her own needs and desires, sometimes naughty, sometimes tender, that she began to feel that she was a mother like any other.

The evidence, however, suggests otherwise. Colette was always a distant mother, intent on pursuing her career as a journalist and writer, on being part of her husband's world of politics and diplomacy. Bel-Gazou never enjoyed the nurturing security of a mother's love that Colette had experienced as a child. She spent the first seven years of her life in the care of the rather formidable, but loved, Miss Draper, 'Nursie dear', as she called her English governess. At the age of nine, she was sent to boarding school and then, when she was twelve, she went to school in England for a year. For a child born into an upper-class family, this was not such an unusual childhood. What was different, however, was a mother who was so occupied with pursuing her many activities that there was so little time for mothering. She even missed her daughter's birthdays.

The situation did not change after the war. When Bel-Gazou returned to Paris to live with her parents, she rarely saw them. As an adult, her memories of her childhood were of her parents being 'at the offices of *Le Matin*, at work, pursuing their own lives. I was just this little nothing in a corridor'. The letters between mother and daughter, entrusted by Bel-Gazou to her niece Anne de Jouvenel, the daughter of Bertrand de Jouvenel, and published in *Lettres à sa fille* (1916–1953) in 2003, reveal a child who longed to see her mother and who waited hopefully for her visits. She was a child who feared that she would never be worthy of her parents' love, and would never meet their expectations.

One of the child's plaintive letters from boarding school begged her mother to come to visit on Thursday afternoon, when all the other mothers visited. 'I waited for you for a long time and finally at six o'clock, when I saw that you were not coming, I thought that you must surely be sick with the flu.' Making excuses for her mother, Bel-Gazou was learning the hard way that she did not have a position of priority in

her mother's busy life. During school holidays, rather than returning home, she often found herself entrusted to friends.

Colette loved her daughter, but in her own way. It was a tough love; a love that set high standards and created a burden of expectation, that wanted to see her daughter succeed rather than waste her talents. The tragedy of Bel-Gazou's life—as indeed Colette herself saw—was that she was the daughter of two famous people. When Bel-Gazou was just ten years old, her mother wrote to her accusing her of lack of character, and of being just like hundreds, even thousands, of other little girls. 'I am waiting for something of your father and of your mother to appear in you. And I find that I am waiting a long time. Do what you can so that this expectation is no longer disappointed.' We didn't bring you into this world, she said in this same long letter, to be just an ordinary little girl, to be mediocre.

Colette had not made her daughter's life any easier by calling her Colette. Even her nickname, Bel-Gazou, was not hers alone. This 'fusion' between mother and daughter, as Anne de Jouvenel calls it, made it extremely difficult for Colette's daughter to establish her own identity, to differentiate herself from her famous mother. When asked what it meant to have such a famous mother, Bel-Gazou answered: 'You need a lifetime to get over it.'

Colette turned more towards her daughter in her later years—acknowledging the distance that she had put between them and yet professing her deep love for her. It was now

Top, Colette and Henry de Jouvenel, in Rome; bottom, Henry de Jouvenel

her turn to ask for letters and visits, just as it had been Sido's fifty years earlier. Jean Cocteau, who was Colette's neighbour and friend in the later years of her life, wrote that Colette intimidated her daughter. 'I always saw mother and daughter calling to each other from afar,' he wrote, 'groping in the dark towards each other, like in a lovers' game of blind-man's buff or hide and seek.'

Colette's visits to Castel-Novel during the war years provided respite from her busy schedule in Paris, and she took great pleasure in playing the role of farmer or farmer's wife. Castel-Novel was a serious farm, with cattle, pigs and a commercial poultry enterprise with chickens, turkeys, guinea-fowl and geese. She enjoyed making jams, separating the milk, moulding fresh cheeses, making her own butter. She even thought of selling apples commercially.

It was a far cry from the deprived conditions being experienced by Parisians and by those living in the war-torn regions of northern France. There was luscious cream, garlic by the cartful, an abundance of peaches and apples, but life was difficult for the women left to manage the farms by themselves. They were on the point of exhaustion, Colette wrote. 'The hay is still in the fields ... the women, bent double under the weight of work and diminished by loneliness, are on the point of giving up. Helping hands are too few and too late.' The children were put to work, 8- and 10-year-olds raking up the hay, working alongside the old men. The old gardener had come back to work on the estate at the age of eighty, presenting a basket of gifts: 'pink radishes and black cherries, artichoke flowers standing stiffly between their two metallic-coloured leaves, strawberries, asparagus bundled up with a bit of reed: the produce of his labour'.

While Jouvenel was at the front at Verdun, Colette was living in Passy, in Paris's 16th arrondissement, in the company of a number of women friends, sharing the household chores, shopping, cleaning and cooking and on those still nights when they could hear the sounds of the cannons to the east of Paris, keeping their spirits up by telling stories.

In December 1914, Colette went clandestinely to the front to see Jouvenel, and she spent Christmas with him. She returned in February of 1915, and again in the middle of May. In her articles for *Le Matin*, as well as in her many letters, she described the weeks she spent there, cloistered during the day and only venturing out at night. There was the relentlessness and horror of life at the front, the devastation, but there was also the courage and humour, the children who scavenged in the debris for toys, for something to eat, the air battles where planes became birds swooping and turning.

In the middle of 1915, Colette was sent to Italy to report on what was happening there now that Italy had declared war against the Austro-Hungarian Empire. Colette continued to write for *Le Matin* until 1916, when she was back in Italy with Jouvenel, who was sent as a delegate to a summit of the Allies. Later that year, Colette was once again in Rome for the filming of *La Vagabonde*, with the actress Musidora in the role of Renée. It was at this time that Colette's interest in the cinema was born. The first writer to pay serious attention to this new art form, she was also one of the first to write about film, reviewing the movies *Civilisation*, directed by Thomas H. Ince, and *Mater Dolorosa*, directed by Abel Gance, for *Le Film* in 1917.

Jouvenel was appointed private secretary to Anatole de Monzie, a deputy from the Lot, but at the end of 1917 he was back at the front. He was to remain there through the tough months that followed, until the armistice was finally declared in November 1918.

Whilst Colette was spared the losses of close family that afflicted so many people, she lost two very close friends in the later years of the war. Leon Hamel, who had been a friend and confidant since 1905 when he had first met Colette, died in April 1917. Hamel, fifteen years older than Colette, was an Orientalist who had travelled extensively through the Far East and had lived in Egypt for seven years. An elegant, extremely discreet man with private means, he had ties with many people in literary and theatrical circles, and it was through these connections that he met Colette. He was a supportive and tactful friend through the tumultuous years of her separation and divorce from Willy, her relationship with Missy and her marriage to Henry de Jouvenel. Colette drew on him for the character of Hamond In *La Vagabonde* and *L'Entrave*.

Then, just as the war was drawing to its close in 1918, her friend Annie de Pène was struck down by Spanish flu, the deadly pandemic that killed millions around

the world. Colette had much in common with Annie, who like her was a writer and journalist. She, too, had a provincial background, and drew on her childhood memories of Normandy in her writing. She had also married young, and had turned to journalism and writing after separating from her husband and moving to Paris. She was the companion of Gustave Téry, the brilliant director of the socialist weekly paper *L'Oeuvre*. Annie de Pène also went to the front during the war, and a collection of her articles was published in 1915 in a small book entitled *Une Femme dans la tranchée* (*A Woman in the Trenches*). The letters between Annie de Pène and Colette reveal a very deep, though short-lived, friendship, which led to a maternal and slightly more troubled friendship with Annie's daughter, Germaine Beaumont, who was herself a writer of some note.

After the war, Henry de Jouvenel returned to his position as editor of *Le Matin*, and Colette was appointed literary editor and then theatre critic. Their professional lives were flourishing but their marriage was unravelling. Jouvenel had taken a younger mistress, Germaine Patat, who ran a successful small fashion house in Paris. She often accompanied Jouvenel when he came to Rozven or to Castel-Novel. As with previous 'other' women in her life, Colette befriended Germaine, who became an integral part of the family and very close to Bel-Gazou. Indeed, Germaine was one of the friends to whom Colette willingly entrusted Bel-Gazou during the school holidays.

There were still times, however, when Colette fulfilled the role of Baroness at Castel-Novel. When Jouvenel was standing for elections in 1921, she accompanied him to race meetings, to dinners and on visits throughout the region after it had been devastated by a cyclone. Jouvenel was elected senator for the Corrèze department, and he embarked on a successful political career.

When Jouvenel learnt of Colette's relationship with her stepson Bertrand, he confronted Colette and insisted that it be brought to an end. Bertrand was to be sent to Prague, where Jouvenel had negotiated a position for him in the embassy. Colette refused to break off the relationship, and thereafter virtually the only contact between Colette and Jouvenel was via lawyers. By this time, Jouvenel was in a relationship with the Romanian princess, Marthe Bibesco. Colette was no longer the physically attractive woman she had been in 1910, when they'd first met, and her past was probably something of an embarrassment to Jouvenel as his political career gained momentum.

In 1923, Jouvenel was appointed as French delegate to the League of Nations, which was based in Geneva, resulting in more absences. At the end of that year,

Colette de Jouvenel

The marriage of Colette de Jouvenel to Doctor Camille Dausse at Castel-Novel

Colette returned to their house in Auteuil to find that Jouvenel had moved out. Colette's days as chatelaine were over. The year 1923 also marked the end of her collaboration with *Le Matin*.

Colette and Jouvenel were divorced in 1925. Jouvenel married for the third time in 1930, marrying the wealthy widow of the successful banker and businessman Charles Louis-Dreyfus. His career as an international diplomat and journalist was to flourish for another ten years, before his sudden death from a heart attack in 1935.

Colette still had news of Castel-Novel through her daughter and stepsons, who returned to the castle regularly for family holidays. As an adult, Colette's daughter tried her hand at many things—film assistant, interior decorator, dealer in antiques—but she never gave herself the chance to succeed in any of them. She was married in 1935, at Castel-Novel but, the marriage was very short-lived. She divorced just a couple of months later, for reasons of 'physical repulsion', as her mother wrote to a friend. Colette did not attend her daughter's wedding. Jouvenel was unlikely to have opposed her presence, but for Colette, it was easier to stay away. Once again, her daughter had to make do without her mother.

The year 1935 was a difficult time for the young Colette de Jouvenel. It was the year of her own ill-fated marriage, and just a few months later, her father met his untimely death. It was also the year of her mother's marriage to her third husband, Maurice Goudeket, which created yet another obstacle between mother and daughter. Young Colette found herself much closer to her father's third wife, and to her Jouvenel family, than to her mother from whom she distanced herself.

During the Second World War, Colette de Jouvenel offered refuge to her mother and Goudeket at Curemonte, near Castel-Novel, in the run-down castle that her half-brother Renaud had made available to her. For Colette, however, this was to be a very brief stay. In letters to friends, Colette described Curemonte as a 'verdant tomb'. They were a whole month without mail, without telegrams, without the telephone and without newspapers. The silence was much more difficult to bear than danger, she wrote. She was impatient to have contact with people, to know what was going on.

The war at last provided Colette de Jouvenel with a raison d'être, and she stayed on at Curemonte, where she gathered around her a group of loyal friends and provided refuge for those in need, including Jewish children. She came into her own, working with the Resistance, writing articles for *Fraternité* and other journals during and after the war, and even setting up a new journal. Her work earned her the respect and appreciation of the local people, who appointed her mayor of the commune in 1944.

Today, Curemonte—just a short drive from Castel-Novel—is a quiet little village that is proud of its rich heritage and of its status as one of the most beautiful villages in France. The castle—actually two castles within a single surrounding wall—stands tall in the middle of the village, encircled by a number of fine houses that date from the sixteenth century, houses that belonged to the officers and others who served the lords at the time. The castle has been restored by its present owners.

The village square was quiet when we were there. A woman was walking past the castle gate, carrying a large basket, and she stopped to have a chat. She was taking food to a sick neighbour. When I told her why I was there, she said that she remembered meeting Colette in the village when she was a young girl, and what a lovely warm person she had been. Was it Colette the mother or Colette the daughter? Probably the daughter, I thought, given the brevity of Colette's stay here during those early years of the war.

At the end of the war, Colette wrote to her daughter expressing her regret that they had not been closer and hoping that her daughter might now find some peace after all she had done during the war. The time comes when you regret having had children late, she wrote. 'I know this to be true, now that I find myself watching you from afar. I embrace you tenderly, my darling, and much as it may not seem so, I am profoundly yours.'

And yet, at this very same time, Colette was effectively disinheriting her daughter. Her will, executed in 1945, left Goudeket all the moral rights relating to her works and half the royalties. Goudeket had sole decision as to all future publications and editions of her work, and was to provide an annual account to Colette de Jouvenel of what was her due. If Bel-Gazou were to contest the will, she would lose the right to the 50 per cent of royalties provided for her in the will. Even in death, Colette caused her daughter ongoing heartache, though the extent to which Goudeket was responsible for this outcome will never be known.

After her mother's death, Colette de Jouvenel spent much of her time outside France. She had a house on Capri and it was there, where neither her mother's nor her father's names were known, that she seemed able to enjoy a happy anonymous life.

Nonetheless, Colette de Jouvenel always acknowledged the achievements of her mother and what she had learnt from her—her rigorous personal ethics, based on an energetic commitment to life in all its forms, and an intolerance of mediocrity—and following the death of Maurice Goudeket in 1977, she dedicated the last years of her life to promoting her mother's fame and glory. She died of cancer in 1981 at the age of only sixty-eight.

❧

The troubled relationship between mother and daughter was never far from my thoughts while I was at Castel-Novel. The woman who had experienced so much love from her own mother that she had had to break free of its grip, in order to lead her own life and become her own person, went to the other extreme with her own daughter. Words could never heal the loneliness and hurt experienced by a young girl who learnt very early that you don't ask questions of a mother who is working.

On our last morning at Castel-Novel, we woke to the sounds of birds and to the mist rising from the valley. A perfect day to visit the nearby floral park called Les Jardins de Colette (Colette's Gardens), established just a few years ago by the local municipality. Here was my journey in the footsteps of Colette in miniature. The garden's meandering path takes the visitor from Saint-Sauveur to Brittany, from Provence to the Palais-Royal. Bel-Gazou's sections of the garden are represented by a labyrinth in the shape of a butterfly and a little farmyard. Is this where Bel-Gazou can finally find her peace with her mother, at Castel-Novel and in the memories of the brief but happy times they spent together here?

For ten years, Castel-Novel had been a cherished retreat for Colette. It was the childhood home of her daughter and it was here that she was best able to indulge a motherly pride in her daughter. The times she shared with Bel-Gazou at Castel-Novel were happy and relaxed. 'She is the model of a perfect child,' Colette wrote to Marguerite Moreno in 1921. She took pride in her daughter's robust little body, with its 'hard little bottom, plump arms, and when she stands up on tiptoes … two fine muscles the shape of hearts in her calves, like those of sailors when they are climbing the rigging'.

For Colette, the Limousin was a country of adoption. It was the landscape that connected her most closely with country life, infusing her letters with the richness of the autumn harvests, the summer profusion of flowers. But most of all, it was the landscape of Bel-Gazou.

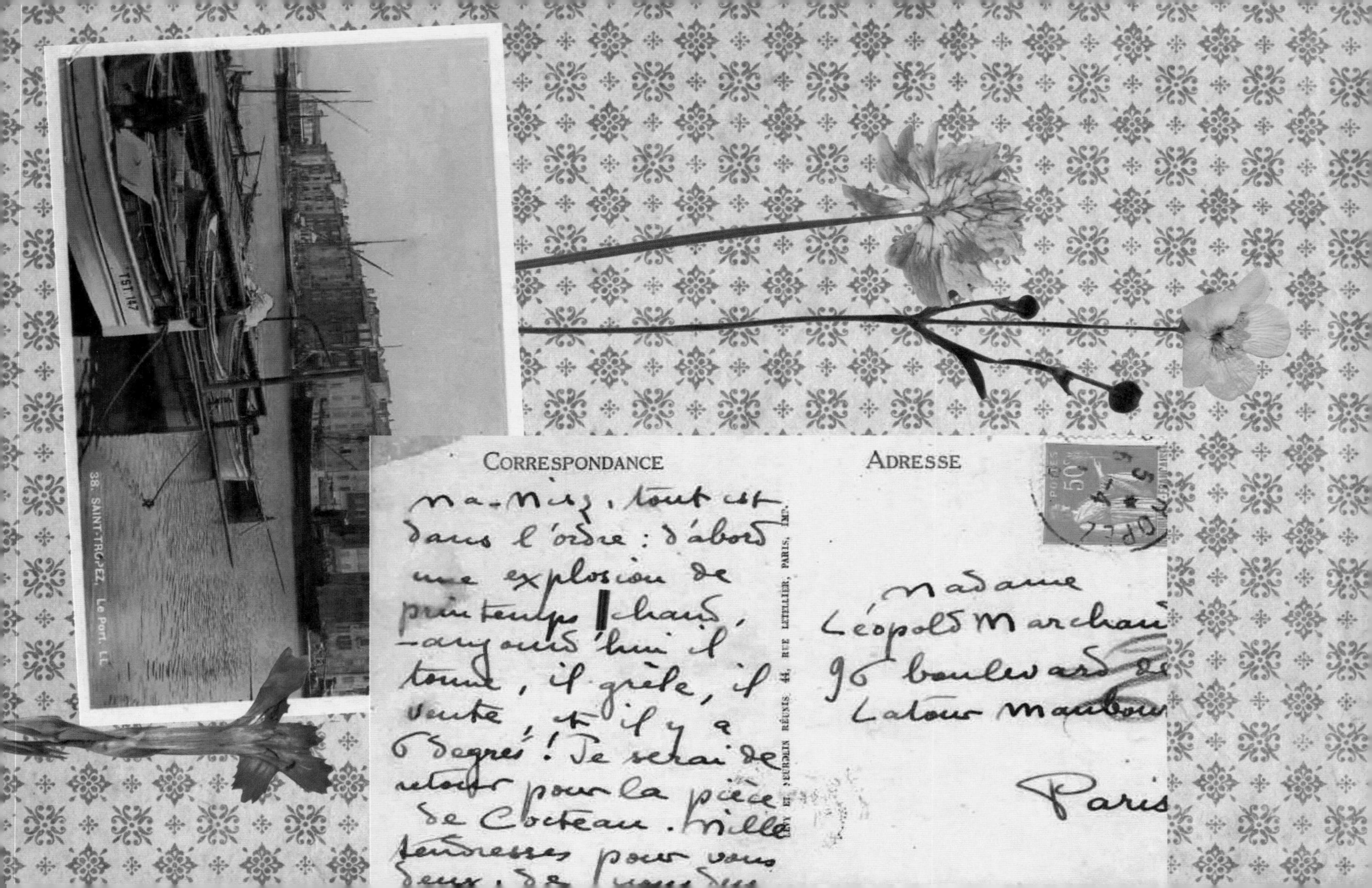

ADRESSE

Madame

Léopold Marchand

96 boulevard S¹

Latour Maubourg

Paris

CORRESPONDANCE

Ma-ma; tout est
dans l'odre : d'abord
une explosion de
printemps ! ans;
aujourd'hui, il
tout, il gèle, il
neige ; ! Je serai de
retour pour la pièce de
Cocteau. Millé
tendresses pour vous
deux. J.B. Pierre bien

38. SAINT-TROPEZ. Le Port. LL

Chapter 7

— Provence — a new love —

We have just passed through Avignon and, when I awoke yesterday from a two-hour nap, it was as though I had slept for two months: spring had appeared on my route, springtime like in fairytales, exuberant, fleeting, irresistible springtime of the South, rich, fresh, bursting out in sudden greenery, in grasses already long, swaying and shimmering in the wind, in mauve Judas-trees, in paulownias the colour of grey periwinkles, in golden chain trees, wisteria and roses!

My friend, I am dazzled and restored by this new season, this severe and bracing sky, the particular golden glow of stones that are caressed by the sun all year long … No, don't pity me for having to leave at dawn, because dawn, in this countryside, emerges from a milky sky, naked and tinged with crimson, fanned by the sound of bells and the flight of white pigeons.

Colette was fifty-two when she met Maurice Goudeket, who was to become her third husband. A chance meeting, over dinner with friends, led to a relationship that would last until her death.

Colette was in her prime. In 1925, her divorce from Jouvenel was finalised. Her reputation as a serious writer was firmly established. She had nurtured many young writers in her role as literary editor for *Le Matin*, and in 1920 she had been named Chevalier of the Legion of Honour.

The war had in many ways liberated women. Coco Chanel was designing an entirely new wardrobe for women that reflected this new liberty. Gone were the corsets and bustles. Women were dressing in supple, easy clothes—clothes for the beach and for playing sport. For many women, Colette represented this newfound freedom and independence. She had written of the struggles of women to be free of the shackles of love; she had claimed for women the freedom to enjoy their own sexuality, to enjoy a life of the senses. She had refused to be constrained by social conventions.

She was performing on the stage again, in dramatic adaptations of her own work, *Chéri* and *La Vagabonde*. 'Anyone who has not seen Colette play in *Chéri*,' wrote one critic, 'has deprived themselves not only of great pleasure, but also of an understanding of this famous novel.' As Léa, he continued, Colette 'lived, breathed, feared, dissimulated, protected and suffered'. Colette was indeed playing from real life. She was still in a relationship with her stepson Bertrand when she first met Goudeket.

A few months after their first meeting, Maurice Goudeket and Colette met for a second time, while visiting friends in the South of France. By happenstance, they shared the trip back to Paris in his car. She sent him a copy of *La Vagabonde*, with a dedication: 'In memory of a thousand kilometres of vagabondage'. At some point over the next few months, they became lovers. This young man is exquisite, she wrote to Marguerite Moreno. He was like a 'covered flame', a 'chic type' with 'a satin skin'. He would be her lover, husband and life-long companion, but never master. Natalie Clifford-Barney had written that Colette liked her men one at a time, so that they could become her master. This relationship would be different.

Maurice Goudeket was a successful dealer in pearls, who had also tried his hand as an author. He had read and admired Colette's work when he was a student, and had written a couple of plays, as well as articles.

Maurice Goudeket

He was reserved, formal and, at the age of thirty-five, still emotionally unattached. On the surface, Goudeket's reserve and Colette's unconventionality would seem to make them the most unlikely of partners, and yet Goudeket was captivated by Colette's energy and passion, she by his 'masculine grace', the satanic charm of his calm exterior.

In June of 1925, Goudeket invited Colette to join him for two weeks in a villa near Sainte-Maxime, just across the bay from Saint-Tropez. Colette was seduced—both by Maurice and by Provence. 'I wander through the crackling brazier of the pine forests, past the melting resins, over the flagstones that burn your bare feet … The sea, the sand are my native element, and so is love,' she wrote to Marguerite Moreno.

Colette decided to sell her house in Rozven and buy a property in the South. When she found La Treille Muscate, it was called Tamaris les Pins. 'A good name for a railway station,' said Colette, who promptly renamed her new domain after the climbing muscat grape that grew near the well. The property was just outside the little fishing village of Saint-Tropez. To find it, she'd had to tear herself away from

the little Mediterranean port, with its 'flat-roofed houses, painted in faded candy pink, lavender blue, linden-tree green, away from the streets where the scent of sliced melons, of nougat and sea-urchins hovers'. It was a simple little house, surrounded by a couple of hectares of land with a small vineyard, an orange grove, fig trees and, just beyond the pine trees, the little coastal path and then the bay.

I had contacted Christine, the home's current owner, in advance of our visit, and arranged to meet her at the house. It had been an overcast day, with spring showers and dark clouds, but towards the end of the afternoon the clouds cleared, and the house and garden glowed in the late-afternoon light. From the terrace in front of what had been Colette's bedroom, we looked out through the trees to catch glimpses of the Baie des Canebiers.

The vines that used to surround the house have been replaced by a grove of cypresses and olive trees. The old well, where Colette kept her bottles of wine cool, is still there and, at the end of the vine-covered arched walkway, the wisteria-shaded porch reminded me that this was where she would set the table and welcome friends for lunch. When the wisteria is in bloom, the light is tinged with mauve, Christine told me. The orange trees were laden with fruit when we visited—small oranges with a bittersweet taste—but only one fig tree remains. The garden is still a profusion of oleanders, which reach their branches out over the front gate and, though the flower

beds have gone, there are flowering vines and rose bushes, including the delicate rose de mai that is used in Chanel's original perfume, No. 5.

When Colette 'discovered' Saint-Tropez, it was already frequented by a lively group of artists and writers, with whom Colette soon became friends. André Dunoyer de Segonzac, Luc-Albert Moreau and André Villeboeuf jointly owned a property called Le Maquis on a nearby hillside. They and other friends became part of a little group that gathered in the summer months. The writer Francis Carco, whom Colette had known since her early days in Paris, and his wife had a house nearby. The violinist Hélène Jourdan-Morhange, who was to become Luc-Albert Moreau's wife and who was a friend and favourite interpreter of Ravel, moved in and out of this convivial group, along with the actress Thérèse Dorny who married Dunoyer de Segonzac, and the critic Régis Gignoux. They would meet on the beach at Camarat, go for drives in the Dom forest, have lunches on the terrace at La Treille Muscate or meet in the evening at one of the little bars in Saint-Tropez. Colette produced her own wine—a rosé, 'the colour of redcurrant', to accompany the green melons; and a white, 'the colour of amber, redolent of warm sand', to go with the salad of tomatoes, peppers, onions, all bathed in oil. Hers was a garden that provided sustenance as well as beauty.

Colette admired her artist friends' ability to capture the colours of the South, and she wrote of the 'respectful envy that we mere scratchers on paper feel for those who work at such close quarters with the rainbow'. She did not hesitate to ask them to illustrate her work. Dunoyer de Segonzac illustrated a deluxe edition of short pieces collected and published as *La Treille Muscate* in 1932. Luc-Albert Moreau illustrated an edition of *La Naissance du jour* (*Break of Day*), also published in 1932.

Colette's friendships with artists extended beyond those she knew in the South, and many of her works were produced in fine illustrated editions. André Dignimont, whom Colette affectionately called 'le grand Dig', illustrated an edition of *La Vagabonde* in 1927 and *l'Ingénue libertine* in 1928. Vertès, Daragnès, Raoul Dufy, even Matisse, were amongst the many artists with whom she worked over the years. She wrote introductions to catalogues of their exhibitions; they illustrated her work.

The period from 1926 to 1938 was one of the most productive of Colette's life. It was a continuation of the return to her past that had started with *La Maison de Claudine* published just a few years earlier.

Colette writing on the vine-covered porch

Sido was now long dead—she'd died in 1912—and with her life now entering a period of peace and tranquillity, Colette could re-engage with this powerful woman, whose possessive love had been both a joy and a burden. It was at La Treille Muscate that she began to sort through and reread her mother's letters.

> *Is this my last house? I take measure of it, listen to it ...*
> *Might I have attained here that which one can never start again? Everything*
> *resembles the first years of my life, and I recognise, bit by bit, in this humble rural*
> *property, in the cats, the old dog ... I recognise the way home ... An ephemeral castle,*
> *melting into the distance, gives way to this little house. Here, when I believed I would*
> *never find it in this life, here, does there exist in fact a garden path where*
> *I can follow my own footprints? At the edge of the well, is that the ghost of my mother,*
> *dressed in an old-fashioned dress of blue satin, filling the watering-cans?*

In 1926, as she grappled with these memories, Colette began writing what was to become one of her greatest novels, *La Naissance du jour*. Like so many of Colette's later works, there is a narrator who calls herself Colette and throughout the book there are extracts of letters from her mother. Is this the reconciliation with the past

Illustration by Dunoyer de Segonzac for La Treille muscate

that she has sought? *'I recognise the way home,'* she writes. Or is this yet another fiction that she is constructing about her life—both present and past? Indeed she warns the reader, 'Do you imagine, as you read, that I am painting my portrait? Patience, it is only my model.'

The book opens with an excerpt taken from a letter from Sido to Colette's second husband. In the letter, she writes that she cannot come to visit because she does not want to miss the flowering of her pink cactus. The narrator goes on to compare herself to this woman, to draw strength from the fact that she is the daughter of this woman who bent over the flowering of a pink cactus and who never ceased, herself, to flower throughout her life. She looks at herself in the mirror and sees how she is coming to resemble her mother as she grows older. She notes the parallels in their lives—she had two husbands, though Colette was of course to have a third. But this letter—as with others in *La Naissance du jour*—is as much Colette's writing as it is her mother's. Indeed, in this first letter, the sense of her mother's letter has been completely changed.

Sido's actual letter to Jouvenel accepted his invitation to visit; she *wanted* to see her daughter, and also to get to know the man with whom Colette had chosen to throw in her lot. In doing so, Sido left behind her cat, as well as a cactus that was about to flower and a gloxinia that was in full flower. In *La Naissance du jour*, Colette was continuing to elaborate on the myth of Sido as the 'goddess mother', a myth that she had started to sketch out in *La Maison de Claudine*. She was creating a mother whose needs were not nearly as demanding as those of her real mother; she was creating the mother she could revere, without feeling guilty. This character reappears throughout the book, the extracts from her letters moulded by Colette to meet her literary needs.

As with so much of her writing, Colette draws not only on her mother's letters for this book, but also on her surroundings and on her own circumstances. The novel is set in Saint-Tropez, and a number of her artist and writer friends appear—real people mingling with fictitious characters. While the book celebrates the natural environment as well as the ease of life in the South, this real world is the point of departure for the work of art which emerges through the act of writing, of creating a symbolic and fictitious world that goes beyond reality. The plot, insubstantial as it is, is a backdrop for Colette's reflections, yet these reflections are those of the 'I' in the narrative, and not necessarily those of Colette. The character in the novel claims to want to live—or die—without her life depending on love. Yet Colette, herself, was in the thrall of a new love affair.

Colette was over fifty when this new relationship began, and she would be in her sixties when she and Goudeket married in 1935. In the intervening period, a time of creative abundance and sensual pleasure for Colette, she was to write many of her finest works: *La Seconde* (*The Other One*) and *Sido* were published in 1929; *Ces plaisirs*, later republished as *Le Pur et l'impur* (*The Pure and the Impure*), in 1932; and *La Chatte* (*The Cat*), in 1933.

Le Pur et l'impur was acknowledged by Colette as one of her most profound works, and one of the most difficult to write. Colette had struggled to find a title for this work—a collection of meditations or reflections on the power of erotic love and those whose lives are imprisoned by it. Its original title, *Ces plaisirs* (*These Pleasures*), was accompanied by an epigraph: 'these pleasures that we lightly call physical'.

The book opens with Colette's description of a glass-ceilinged studio in a building somewhere in Paris, where she has been invited by a fellow journalist and writer. Chinese drapes cover the walls, red lamps glow dimly in the alcoves, kimono-clad guests relax on little Japanese mattresses. Refusing the offer of opium, Colette settles down on one of the little mattresses, observing, listening, aware of the 'dark aroma of opium smoke, like fresh truffle or burnt cocoa'. A woman begins to sing in a husky, sweet voice. Someone asks her to continue, but an angry male voice interrupts. 'No, she didn't come here to sing. She is here with me and it is no one else's business.' Later, Colette hears, in the gallery above her, the same sweet voice trying to hold off her pleasure, and then hastening it towards its climax, like the song of a nightingale. Through a chance second encounter, Colette learns that this public display had been carefully staged, as this woman's gift to a needy young man. 'This veiled face of a subtle woman,' Colette wrote, 'without illusion, skilled in deception and in tact, is a fitting introduction to this book which will speak sadly of pleasure.'

Colette goes on to recall other 'phantoms who have come and gone in my life, troubled and still suffering from having run, headlong or sideways, onto the incomprehensible and hidden reef, that is the human body'. She writes of the links between physical and emotional dependencies. Sexual and physical pleasure is a searching for fulfilment, but this search is an insatiable hunger. Whether it is between man and woman or between two women, the quest for completeness is illusory. There is only the void of solitude, and it is in this solitude that one must find one's strength and one's ability to give and accept pleasure. Hunger and greed lead only to more of the same, and to the sense of always being cheated.

The habit of sensual pleasure, although less tyrannical than that of tobacco, nonetheless becomes addictive … It is perhaps the only misplaced curiosity, that which insists on knowing, on this side of death, that which lies just beyond life.

Beyond greed and beyond desire lies peace, but not necessarily purity. 'Purity' was a word that had no intellectual meaning for Colette; she could only assuage her thirst for it in its visual evocations—'in air bubbles, in deep water, and in the unattainable, fortressed sites at the centre of a thick crystal ball'. And just as there was no 'pure', nor was there an 'impure'. Sin, and particularly original sin, had no meaning for Colette. What was 'impure' was the failure to be true to oneself and to the respect one owed to all living creatures.

This was a very personal book, one in which Colette talked about her own domination by her senses, about being consumed with jealousy, about the pleasure of being able to wound, about the shame of living a life of pretence. With Goudeket, Colette had finally met a man to whom she did not feel she had to submit, nor did she have to dominate. Theirs was a pleasure both physical and emotional, and it gave Colette a sense of freedom and wellbeing. 'It is only when one is better,' she wrote to Maurice, 'that one discovers one wasn't very well.'

As she had previously written in *La Naissance du jour*, she was retreating from the battleground of love, the place of addiction and submission, to a place of friendship and peace. 'Love, one of the great banalities of life, is withdrawing from my life.' Colette was fashioning her last mask, the mask of a woman who lives within the plenitude of a life of the senses, a narcissistic mask where she was at peace, in the centre of a world peopled by her own memories and her own creations.

Like her artist friends, Colette worked when she was at La Treille Muscate. Dunoyer de Segonzac, who was working on a series of sketches of her, described the rhythm of her days. Gardening in the morning before meeting friends on the beach, and then lunch in the trellised shade of the porch. After lunch, the cats would be called for their walk, forming a procession behind her along the pathways bordered by flowers and herbs. Then a brief siesta before finally settling down in the downstairs room at a small fold-out Provençal writing desk, which she had placed facing the corner of the room, so as to avoid all distractions. She would stay there for several hours, completely focused, the silence broken only by the crumpling of a page

'Are you for or against the 'second job' of a writer?'

Etes-vous pour, ou contre
le "second métier" de l'écrivain?
Colette

6, rue de
Miromesnil

VILLA DE MADAME COLLETTE !'

9948 — SAINT-TROPEZ (Var).

Annotations by Colette on a postcard she found on sale, much to her disgust, in the newsagent at Saint-Tropez

that she rejected with controlled rage. Towards evening she would suddenly get up, announcing, 'Enough for today!' She would call out to Maurice, throw a shawl around her shoulders and head off, surrounded by her animals, to meet friends at the port.

Throughout the 1930s, Colette's letters record the delight she continued to find each year as she returned to her Provençal retreat, no matter what the season. She described the mistral, 'magnificent, green and pink', the 'copper and acid blue of dawn', the 'dark pink of the sunset'. Saint-Tropez was charming in the winter, she wrote to Marguerite Moreno. 'Boutiques become village-like again, papier-mâché dolls, smoked herrings.'

But Saint-Tropez was changing. It had been discovered by the holidaymakers and trendsetters and, in summer at least, its days as a quiet little fishing village were over. 'Saint-Tropez, so my neighbours tell me, is uninhabitable this year,' she wrote to Marguerite Moreno in 1930. She was accosted by people as she came out of shops. The port was blocked with rows of expensive sports cars.

When the summer crowds retreated, however, the silence and solitude returned. 'At dawn, the path along the coast and the hoar-frost of thick dew remain faithful. It is the hour when the dog knows that she doesn't have to have a collar and that she mustn't bark, the clandestine hour.' Large grey-and-pink moths filled the garden at dusk. Swallows nested in the caretaker's little cottage. Geckos sunned themselves on the walls.

For Maurice Goudeket, who struggled to keep his business interests afloat during the Depression, these were challenging years, but his constancy to Colette did not waver. His pearl broking business failed and he tried his hand at various other business schemes in the following years, including being actively involved in Colette's short-lived venture into the beauty products business in 1932. Colette had thrown herself enthusiastically into this new project, in spite of the incredulity of many of her friends and indeed her readers. She had always been interested in perfume and make-up, and she was looking for a change. Writers who do nothing but write become uninteresting and lose touch with what is going on, she commented. She had been a writer and a performer, a writer and journalist—why not a writer and a producer of beauty products? Her name alone would sell them. So, she developed her range of products, wrote her own promotional material, opened a shop in rue de Miromesnil in Paris and enjoyed doing the make-up herself for some of her famous clients.

Maurice and Colette worked hard at the business over the next twelve months, but she was not to escape her destiny as a writer so easily. The business struggled financially and Colette juggled writing commitments and promotional activities until, twelve months later, she decided that the beauty business was not for her.

Over the next few years, lecture tours took Colette as far afield as Austria, Romania and North Africa, as well as throughout France. Maurice and Colette were invited on a cruise to Norway on board a yacht belonging to Henri de Rothschild. In 1935, they sailed on the maiden voyage of the cruise ship *Normandie* to New York, Colette as reporter for *Le Journal*. It was because of this trip that Colette and Goudeket were married, ten years after they had first met, as they had been advised that they would not be able to share a hotel room in New York unless they were husband and wife.

All of these experiences were recorded in articles and essays, many of which were subsequently published in various collections. In 1933, Colette became chief drama critic for *Le Journal*, and between 1934 and 1938 four volumes of her criticism were published under the title *La Jumelle noire* (*The Black Opera Glasses*). Through her deep friendships with people involved in the theatre and her own work on the stage, both as a performer and author, Colette was a passionate participant in and observer of the theatrical world. Her theatre criticism was remarkable for its personal approach, her curiosity and interest in everything that was new, her loyalty to friends and colleagues, and her strength of conviction.

Colette was also receiving greater public acclaim, and her work was praised by many of her peers. She was elected to the Belgian Royal Academy of French Language and Literature in 1935, assuming the seat left vacant by the death of the poet Anna de Noailles. The following year, she was appointed a Commander of the Legion of Honour. Around her, the world of international and national politics played out its inexorable march towards war, but Colette's focus remained on the smaller things of life—the personal, the natural, that which was within reach of hand and heart.

❧

The continuing transformation of Saint-Tropez from sleepy fishing village to fashionable resort finally drove Colette away. In 1938, she sold La Treille Muscate to the actor Charles Vanel. Two years later, without having set foot in it, Vanel sold the property to the current owner's great-grandmother.

When the new owners moved in after the war, it was just as Colette had left it. Crumpled sheets of her blue writing paper still lay in the fireplace; a bust of Colette, probably sculpted by one of her many artist friends, sat in the corner of the downstairs room where she used to write, as it still does today. The property has passed down through the generations of this family who have enjoyed it over the decades, in spite of the many changes that have occurred around them. The property was subdivided and two houses built on the land beyond the original stone wall, where previously there had been only the gardener's cottage, but the house is still surrounded by a hectare of land.

The coastal pathway where Colette used to take her morning walks, picking figs from the trees still dripping with dew, is now lined with houses, and only the occasional hardy fig tree remains clinging to the edge of the path. But the water at Les Salins, Colette's favourite swimming beach, still has the transparent blue she so loved. The little beach is protected between a flat outcrop of rocks at one end and the sweep of the headland at the other. Despite the restaurant overlooking the beach, and the ubiquitous beach lounges and umbrellas for hire, this little cove of beach is still delightfully peaceful.

We drove back into Saint-Tropez, to the hotel where we were staying right on the place des Remparts, overlooking the old port where the fishermen would beach their flat-bottomed boats. The hotel has been in the same family since it opened as a little bar in 1938. After the war, it was frequented by the musicians and writers who flocked to Saint-Tropez—Boris Vian, Juliette Gréco, Françoise Sagan. And then, in 1956, it was Brigitte Bardot's turn with her then husband, Roger Vadim, when he filmed *And God Created Woman* here.

Just a couple of minutes away is the main port, lined with mega-yachts and cafes full of tourists. But in the old port area, with its narrow streets and little squares, it is still possible to experience the charm of Saint-Tropez that captivated Colette almost a century ago. The tiny fish market, with its mosaic decoration, is nestled under the tower of the old fortifications. Just next door is the place aux Herbes, where the tiniest fruit and vegetable market can be found every morning.

We happened to be in Saint-Tropez for the annual *bravade*, which celebrates the patron saint of Saint-Tropez and the courage of the Tropéziens in the face of the enemy. The sound of fifes and drums drew us outside early on our first morning. The old town was bedecked in red-and-white flags, and in all the shop windows were little wooden statues of Saint-Tropez. The *bravade* marched past, a procession of sailors and musketeers, old men and young boys alike, followed by women and girls dressed in Provençal traditional dresses, with wide-brimmed straw hats and patterned shawls. They paraded into the little square where they were received by the mayor in front of the town hall. The statue of Saint-Tropez had been returned to the church. All was safe for another year.

On our last morning in Saint-Tropez, the mistral was blowing. This strong, cold wind that comes from the north was whipping up the sea. The plastic sheeting protecting the terrace of our hotel, where we were having breakfast, was being beaten like a drum by the wind. Overnight, the sunny spring weather of the previous afternoon had been transformed, and the sea and sky were grey and threatening. I walked around the windswept ramparts with sea spray whipping up into my face. The narrow streets were deserted; it was as though Saint-Tropez had wanted to show me all its colours and moods.

After the war, Colette never returned to Saint-Tropez. Nonetheless, she still visited the South of France, staying as the guest of Prince Pierre of Monaco in Monte Carlo or with Charles and Charlotte (Pata) de Polignac in a villa they rented south of Grasse, the centre of the perfume industry in France. Colette's description of the area around Grasse, with its fields of flowers, is a hymn to its perfumes and colours. She described the smell of jasmine that, in the evening, seemed to block the roads 'like a tightened rope'. At night, if there was no moon, she could see 'little constellations of flowers, white amongst the dark foliage'.

The South would never lose its attraction for Colette, but, increasingly immobilised by the arthritis in her hip, she would never again walk along the coastal pathway, nor pick the figs that grew on the old fig tree by the sea.

If you could see the figs on the trees! An old fig tree near the sea had been cut back till just about all that was left was the trunk. From the trunk sprouted a fine display of leaves and figs in profusion … they are bursting out of their skin; at seven o'clock in the morning it is a feast for the gods.

À ceux qui reste

A PARI

par COLETTE

Armée qui part, population civile qui gagne la province, au total, foule de grande raison, et de petit bruit, jamais Paris ne se montra plus calme. Chacun s'émerveille de l'obligeance, du sang-froid de son voisin, et ne pense pas que le voisin lui voue la même estime. Les situations extrêmes forcent, d'un trait sincère et appuyé, presque toutes nos caractéristiques ; qui eût dit que le Français, appelé par la pire urgence, était avant tout un ange de modération? Il l'est pourtant. L'admirable organisation qui dirige le mouvement militaire d'un pays entier n'a pas, seule, droit à notre applaudissement. En France, le plus minime rouage sait se faire intelligent, quand il le veut. Il le veut, en ce moment, de toutes ses forces. La

grande main puissante qui le mène, de quel jeu huilé il la seconde ! Gares et garages emplis puis vidés, départs massifs d'enfants, trains et convois militaires qui s'ébranlent à l'heure dite, efficace célérité des aides bénévoles, diapason modéré des appels et des adieux, quelle dignité dans un tel exode, quel air de sagesse et de précoce expérience...

LE meilleur de Paris a quitté Paris élargi soudain et sonore. Une vie nouvelle, incertaine, commence pour ceux qui restent. Aux obstinés qui virent la guerre de 1914 et prétendent ne rien perdre de « celle-ci », il incombe de renoncer à ce qui peut leur de-

meurer, au cœur, ú tain romantisme prudence. Une d'espiéglerie c maint d'entre nou priser les abris les raids aériens, loir suivre du pourchassé par les rayons croisés des teurs, un vol d'av y eut aussi, parmi braves gens entêt ris, une floraiso crète de « mots re »...

N'imiterons-n la réserv viennent trer, en nos cadets ?

La guerre éch n'est pas de mots qui vaudront le de guerre ».

Chapter 8
— The Palais-Royal — another war in Paris —

Yes, I have found yet another provincial home in Paris; they will always exist for those who care enough to find them ...

Colette moved into her first-floor apartment in the Palais-Royal in 1938. This was to be her last home. There were to be no more castles, no more holiday houses in Saint-Tropez, in Brittany. Her world was becoming more and more confined, held within the arcades that surrounded the Jardin du Palais-Royal, her final garden.

Colette was already familiar with the arcades and gardens of the Palais-Royal. She had visited as a child, with her father, to go to the theatre. From 1926 to 1930, she had lived in one of the mezzanine floor apartments above the passage du Perron, 9 rue de Beaujolais. There she had found herself 'enclosed by the curve of a rainbow', the arched window frame of these mezzanine apartments. This was her 'tunnel', her 'drainpipe', her 'lair cowering under the arcades, squashed between the regal first floor above and the shops below'.

After four years in her 'tunnel', Colette heeded the advice of her doctor and found somewhere to live that was lighter, warmer and more airy. She moved first of all to Claridge's on the Champs-Élysées, and then to an apartment building, the Immeuble Marignan, also on the Champs-Élysées. But in 1938, she was back again in the Palais-Royal, in the apartment she had coveted, accompanied by Maurice and her faithful servant, Pauline, who had started working for Colette in 1915. Just a few months earlier, in an interview with a newspaper journalist, Colette had mentioned how she had long coveted the apartment above her old 'lair'. The day after the article appeared, she received a letter from the occupant. He would be happy to 'cede' the apartment to her.

Colette was welcomed back by many of the residents; one sent her some baked pears, the little bistro opposite sent up pancakes, the antique dealer came to greet her and to offer incense sticks. The owners of a nearby restaurant were old acquaintances, whom she had known when they ran a restaurant on the Left Bank on rue du Cherche-Midi.

The Palais-Royal was built in the seventeenth century as Cardinal Richelieu's palace. It passed to the monarchs after his death, and was the childhood home of Louis XIV. During the eighteenth century, it was in the hands of the Dukes of Orléans, and in the period leading up to, during and after the French Revolution, it was a centre of political intrigue as well as of gambling and prostitution. It was

A new uncertain life begins for those who have stayed …'

here that the revolutionary leader Camille Desmoulins leapt to his feet, flourishing in the air a leaf from one of the chestnut trees. This was to become the badge or cockade of the revolution. And it was also here, just a few years later, that a young girl purchased a heavy kitchen knife before making her way across the Seine to the rue des Cordeliers, where she stabbed the radical journalist and politician Jean-Paul Marat to death as he sat in his bath.

Colette reflected on this colourful past. 'The Palais-Royal,' she wrote, 'is more famous for having been a place of ill repute than for having cradled the Revolution.' The mezzanine apartment where she once lived had probably been the abode of one of those women of the night, she speculated. They were given the name of 'beaver or half-beaver, depending on whether the business profits allowed them to be tenants of a whole or half window'.

But the present fascinated Colette much more than the past. She found the history of the Palais-Royal 'a stale incense' compared with the perfume of roses and freshly watered lawns. She was much more interested in the fact that her friend Marguerite Moreno had lived nearby than that this had been the domain of kings and revolutionaries.

When Colette lived here, it was a somewhat hidden part of Paris, inhabited by artists and actors, with an eccentric collection of shops and craftspeople—hat-makers, shoemakers and stamp dealers. Today, through the inevitable process of gentrification, these businesses are regrettably being replaced by upmarket boutiques and chic little cafes. Nonetheless, it is usually by chance that people happen upon this secret garden in the heart of Paris, with its old-world charm and elegant symmetrical arcades.

On her first morning in her new apartment, Colette imagined she was waking to a fine country morning. The 'sound of a gardener's rake mingled with the wind rustling through the leaves' and the 'liquid cooing' of pigeons. Colette had found her provincial village in the heart of Paris. Her neighbours greeted her as they looked out their windows; the bookseller recounted what had happened in the years since Colette had last lived there. She quickly adjusted to this neighbourhood life, greeting her neighbours, taking an afternoon cup of infusion down into the garden to sit in the sun, with her back against a warm pillar, using a chair as a table.

War was to change this peaceful existence. In 1940, the household fled as the German army advanced on Paris, and they sought refuge at Curemonte with Colette's daughter. Colette and Maurice felt out of touch with what was happening in Paris but, not one to sit about idly, Colette put this period of isolation to good use, writing most of *Journal à rebours* (*Looking Backwards*).

Just a few months later, once the Vichy government was installed over a defeated France, Colette was anxious to get back to the Palais-Royal. 'I am used to living out my wars in Paris,' she wrote, and after a number of setbacks, she and Maurice returned to the city in September 1940, three months after they had fled. Reassuringly, she wrote to her daughter, saying that she, like Colette, would find Paris very beautiful without cars. 'The city is spacious, legible, extremely arresting.' The silence of the city at night was broken only in the early morning by the sound of church bells and the fog horns of the barges on the Seine.

The need to earn a living became even more urgent during the war years, as Maurice, who was of Jewish descent, was not able to work. Colette wrote a number of articles for *Marie-Claire*, which had been launched in 1937, including two special editions for which she was editor-in-chief, in January 1939 and May 1940. In the early months of the war, she encouraged women as they took on new tasks, managing businesses, farming, bringing up the children by themselves, doing the jobs that had previously been men's, while they were away at the front.

After the fall of Paris in June 1940, the situation was very different. Her articles now focused on the challenges of finding food, of keeping warm, of making do. She gave practical advice—recipes where two eggs would be as good as four, where milk could be replaced by water, sugar by salt and a bit of grated cheese. She described the queues of people waiting to go to the theatre, the young women getting up in the dark to walk to work because the clocks had been put back to German time, people reading at the bookstores while eating their lunch. These articles were published in the newspaper *Le Petit Parisien* during 1941, and subsequently collected together in *Paris de ma fenêtre* (*Paris from My Window*) in 1942.

Running through these articles was what Colette called 'a discreet and passive resistance'. She had witnessed one summer morning a man who was cleaning out his birdcages when a German in civvies came into the garden. The newcomer addressed the man with the birdcages in a courteous manner, without a trace of accent, commenting that he seemed to be very happy at his task. 'Oh yes,' the man responded, 'it is early, the gardeners aren't here yet to harass me. I can do my task in peace and tranquillity.' But aren't you aware that the German army is in Paris, asked the man in civvies. 'I understand what you are saying to me,' the man with the birdcages replied, 'but I am not obliged to believe you.' When the newcomer insisted that he had just seen

German troops in the place de l'Opéra, the man responded by stating once again that he had asked him nothing. And as the German left the garden, the man with the birdcages started to whistle a happy little tune. 'It is thus,' wrote Colette, 'in its courteous, cunning and obstinate way, that the Palais-Royal began its resistance and learnt how to keep it up.'

It was from her window that she witnessed 'Paris plunge into sorrow, darkened with remorse and humiliation, but also each day refuse just a little bit more …' She observed the 'unanimous refusal, that emanated from each stone, from each passer-by, from each woman sitting next to her pram … an intense, solid refusal, blind, deaf and mute … A refusal to smile, to be seduced, to be terrorised. Those who were crafty, those who broke into the homes, those who used violence, Paris refused them all.'

In the middle of the night in December 1941, this violence broke into Colette's home when Maurice was arrested. One of a thousand prominent Jewish Parisians arrested in retaliation for the activities of the Resistance, he was held in barracks at Compiègne, and Colette had only occasional news of his fate.

In January 1942, she wrote to one of her friends about the fact that she had not been able to make contact with Goudeket in any way. She was knocking on doors, but the only people who were being evacuated from Compiègne were the seriously ill. She was hoping that she might be able to get a letter through to him, or maybe some food. In the meantime, all she could do was wait.

When I came across this letter in the library in Paris, I was deeply moved. I had known of Goudeket's arrest, but here, in Colette's own handwriting, were the very words she had written during those fateful weeks as she waited for news. I had not previously seen this letter in any of her published correspondence. Seventy years later, and just a few steps away from where it had been written, the letter bore witness to her pain and anxiety, tempered by her indomitable stoicism. Colette did not complain, she did not weep or wail, but she did not hesitate to do all she could to have Goudeket released.

Finally, with the help of various influential friends, including the wife of the German ambassador, Colette succeeded. Two months after he had been taken away, Maurice returned, thin, sallow and covered in mud. Colette then wrote to her dear friend Marguerite Moreno, explaining that she hadn't written because she had been 'carrying a very heavy burden these last eight weeks. Maurice, "absent" since the 12th of December, has just been returned to me. I hadn't wanted to tell you; what was the point of burdening you with this worry. I held on to an obstinate sense of

Maurice and Colette reviewing a manuscript

Colette, framed by the half-moon arch of the window in the Palais-Royal entresol apartment

hope. Now, I am offering myself the luxury of being very tired.'

Once he had recovered his health, Maurice stayed on in Paris until the rounds of mass arrests and deportations began just a few months later in the middle of 1942. Colette and he feared for his safety in Paris, and he managed to travel south to the Free Zone on forged papers. He spent a number of months living with friends in Saint-Tropez, but the end of 1942 brought new dangers. Jews were no longer safe in the Free Zone, so Maurice left Saint-Tropez and took refuge with friends in the Tarn, a remote area in south-west France.

Colette was anxious and becoming increasingly depressed as the war dragged on, so Maurice decided to risk his life to return to Paris to be with her. For the rest of the war, Goudeket lived in Paris, taking refuge every night in various different locations in the Palais-Royal—in maids' rooms, in the bookshop downstairs.

In January 1943, Colette turned seventy. X-rays taken just before the outbreak of war had revealed that she had rheumatoid arthritis in both hips. She was crippled by pain and rarely moved from the apartment. Nonetheless, she continued to work

Entering the apartment at 9 rue de Beaujolais, about 1939

prodigiously and published a number of novellas during the war years. She described her writing at this time as fulfilling 'the mission of the poet: to forget reality, to promise the world miracles, to sing of victory and to deny death'.

Gigi certainly fell into this category. Written in 1942, it recounted the story of a young girl brought up in a world that was familiar to Colette's readers— of courtesans, of performers, of idle wealthy young men. Gigi is being groomed by her aunt in the arts of being a demi-mondaine. She is learning about the value of jewels, how to eat roasted ortolans, bones and all, how to pour coffee. But Gigi knows her own value and sticks to her principles. She is in love with Gaston but refuses to be his mistress. When he returns to ask for her hand, a Cinderella-like happy ending is provided for Colette's readers, who were living through the misery of war.

This light and frothy novella met with resounding success. It was published first in serial form in late 1942, then in 1944 in book form in Lausanne and, after the liberation of Paris in 1945, by one of her prewar publishers, Ferenczi. An American edition came out the following year; stage and screen adaptations followed. 'I have to recognise that with *Gigi*, I touched a nerve,' Colette wrote in February 1954, looking back on its success.

But as the war dragged on, life became increasingly difficult and the horrors of war bore down on friends and family. Friends were arrested; two of Colette's Jewish friends committed suicide; and Colette worried about her daughter and Renaud, as well as others, who were increasingly involved with the Resistance. Two of her younger friends were dying of incurable diseases. Her brother Léo had died in early 1940, the last link with her family now gone. And there were no longer any animals in a household that had always had pets. The last cat, known simply as La Chatte, had died just before the war, followed shortly thereafter by Souci, the last little French bulldog. Colette was not to have any more animals.

Finding food was always a challenge, and Colette was very grateful to a number of friends who kept her well supplied during those difficult years. Her daughter was able to get food parcels to her from Curemonte, as were her two friends whom she called 'the little farmers', who regularly sent her food parcels from Nantes. Gaston Baheux, who was known as Tonton of Montmartre, and who was a close friend of Marguerite Moreno, proved to be a source of delicacies—ham and Gruyère, pigeons, eggs and butter. Tonton ran a series of cabaret restaurants in Montmartre, the most famous of which was Le Liberty's at 5 place Blanche, which he opened in 1940. Le Liberty's was frequented by various artists including Mistinguett, Josephine Baker, Maurice Chevalier, Francis Carco, Jean Cocteau and others. Many young singers got their first break at Le Liberty's, which continued to flourish until it closed its doors for the last time in 1956.

The bookseller and collector Richard Anacréon was another source of provisions during the war. He swapped manuscripts, artwork and first editions for legs of lamb and other victuals, thus keeping artists and writers supplied with food. If you had money, there was clearly food to be found. In this way, Anacréon established an outstanding collection which he bequeathed to Granville, the town where he was born in lower Normandy.

A museum has been established to house his collection, and I had the good fortune to visit Granville when the museum was holding an exhibition dedicated to Colette. It drew extensively on Anacréon's collection, including his beautifully bound and illustrated special editions of Colette's work.

❧

The war was inevitably drawing to a close.

> *Fifteen hundred days, as many days and nights as it takes for a child to be born, to grow up, to learn to speak and to become a delightful and intelligent human being; enough days for accomplished and flourishing people to descend, in frightening numbers, into death … Supported by a hunted companion, and then deprived of this very companion when he was imprisoned, I joined the crowd of women who waited.*

Slowly, rumours started to lighten people's hearts. Paris was already overflowing with hidden men, Colette wrote, with allies. The rumours were growing louder, and then the people of Paris started to call out the names of the leaders who were advancing towards the city. 'At every window, threadbare and badly dyed, cut out and sewn together in the dark and in danger, flags fluttered like foliage.'

The bombing attacks grew more numerous, the sky was full of planes. 'The rectangular expanse of sky over the Palais-Royal framed extraordinary spectacles,' she wrote in 1944 to her daughter. At ground level, the sharpshooters were the most sinister, along with the German tanks that continued to fire in the narrow streets nearby. German soldiers surrendered in the courtyard of the Palais-Royal. Maurice, who went out to see the fighting, was caught in the Tuileries gardens. He was forced to lie low in the gardens for three days, unable to leave as the sharpshooters fired on anything that moved. Colette was frantic with worry and had people out looking for him amongst the dead. She welcomed her husband home with a string of insults.

It had been a long war—one that had cost France and the French dearly. Colette had resisted in her own way. Some would later accuse her of being too close to the occupying forces, of publishing in what was a censored press. She would claim that she had to live and it was only by writing that she could earn a living. Some of her friends were close to the Germans and she used those friendships when she was in dire need. But throughout the war, she remained her own person, beholden to no one and committed to keeping up her own spirits and those of her readers. She embodied the spirit of survival and it was for this that she was recognised. But she had no illusions. She knew that both sacrifice and compromise had played their part in her own survival and in that of the French people.

Francis Carco, her long-time colleague, captured this quality in the preface to *Paris de ma fenêtre* when it was first published in 1944:

> Yes, I believe that this book needed to be written—and indeed by a woman—to pass on to us this lesson of greatness in Paris's proud, daily acceptance. The miracle is that, without a false note, Colette has revealed to us so much fervour, grace, humour, good sense and dignity.

The last cat, who never wanted any other name than La Chatte

COLETTE

AU BORD DE CE JARDIN

A PASSE

SES DERNIERES ANNEES

CARTE POSTALE

UTILISEZ LA P
AERIEN

SE RENSEIGNER DANS
LES BUREAUX DE POSTE

DANS CETTE MAISON

COLETTE

A VECU DE 1927 A 1929 ET
DE 1932 JUSOU A SA MORT
LE 3 AOUT 1954

Chapter 9
— The Blue Lantern —

I am rocking at anchor, under the blue lantern, which is nothing but a strong commercial light at the end of a long extendable arm, dressed with a blue paper shade. Motionless, it nonetheless whispered to my neighbours, the name with which they baptised it, the name of the lantern that ploughs the sea.

The years after the war brought great glory and honour to Colette. She was elected to the Académie Goncourt in May 1945, and four years later was elected President by her fellow members. The Académie Goncourt met on the first Tuesday of every month in the salon Goncourt at the Restaurant Drouant. Each year, the members of the Académie were responsible for choosing the recipient of the Prix Goncourt, the most coveted literary prize in France, awarded for the best and most imaginative prose work of the year.

Colette enjoyed her regular lunches at the Restaurant Drouant with her fellow academicians. As the only woman, she admitted to a very feminine pleasure, being surrounded by an assembly of men. None of them had lost the love of writing nor the love of writers. What else would have kept them going, reading a hundred or more new novels every year, conscientious and aware of the responsibility of choosing one to be the recipient of the prize.

'The evening papers recount our difficult choice in three amusing lines,' she wrote. ' "Helped along by the traditional oysters and the famous *blanc de blancs*, once again the members of the Goncourt are in agreement ..." But no, no, it is not as easy as that, the hour of white wine and the vote.'

The members of the Académie Goncourt still meet at the same restaurant. We went there for lunch one day, and at the end of our meal I chatted to one of the staff about my interest in Colette and the Académie. We were invited to go upstairs to see the salon where the Académie meets.

I recognised the room from the photos I had seen. Portraits of the two nineteenth-century writers and chroniclers of Paris, the Goncourt brothers, Edmond and Jules, have pride of place between the windows that look out on the little place Gaillon. It was Edmond who established the Académie and its prize in his will, to honour the memory of his brother Jules. Since 1903, the ten members of the Académie have met monthly at the large oval table. Ten dining chairs, upholstered with gold velvet, surround the table. On the back of each is engraved the name of one of the current ten academicians. Their initials are also engraved, we are told, on each member's

Enjoying oysters and white wine at the Prix Goncourt luncheon

individual set of cutlery. Traditions are still upheld. When a member dies, his or her place is set for the next monthly lunch. As the meal progresses, the setting is removed piece by piece, until at the end of the meal there remains just a single red rose.

The restaurant is proud of its historical and contemporary literary associations. Downstairs, the bar is adorned with photos of stars of the stage and screen, as well as of writers. The jury of the Prix Renaudot also meets here in its own salon, and there is a small salon Colette, which seats two people for intimate lunches or dinners.

℀

Maurice Goudeket was increasingly managing Colette's affairs. He was working with her to finalise the publication of her complete works, the first of fifteen volumes having been published in 1948. Her works were now reaching a wider audience, through film and the theatre. *Gigi* was made into a film in France in 1949 and then, in 1951, Anita Loos, the American author of *Gentlemen Prefer Blondes*, wrote a

Jean Cocteau and Colette in the Palais-Royal gardens

theatrical adaptation in English for Broadway. On one of her visits to Monte Carlo, Colette happened to see Audrey Hepburn, who was filming there. Colette was immediately captivated by her ingénue looks. 'There's our Gigi for America,' she said to Maurice. The Broadway production was a great success, and in 1959 a film version with Leslie Caron as Gigi was produced in Hollywood.

Theatrical and film productions of other works followed in the years from 1950.

Colette with Audrey Hepburn

Chéri, *La Seconde* and *Gigi* were presented in theatres in Paris. There were films of *Chéri*, *Julie de Carneilhan* and *Minne, L'Ingénue libertine*. In 1950, Yannick Bellon's documentary *Colette* was premiered. Colette is depicted reigning supreme over her little domain in the Palais-Royal. Her faithful housekeeper, Pauline, brings her breakfast and Maurice joins her. They talk about the film that is being made. There are flashbacks to the garden in Saint-Sauveur, to her life as a pantomime artist with her old friend Georges Wague, who said that, just as Colette wrote like no one else, it was thus

with her mime performances. Pauline returns from the market, and Colette, ever the gourmand, admires and tastes the vegetables and fruit in her shopping basket. Jean Cocteau, her neighbour in the Palais-Royal, comes to visit and sits at the end of her bed. They talk about the difficulty of writing. But you make it seem so easy he says. The 77-year-old Colette is being coquettish. 'Oh no,' she says, batting her eyelids, when he talks about the fifty books she has published, 'that is frightening.' And they go on to talk about laziness—something that has tempted them both, but to which neither has succumbed.

In 1954, Claude Autant-Lara's film of *Le Blé en herbe* (*The Ripening Seed*) was premiered. Thirty years after the book's first publication, it still caused a scandal amongst parents and teachers, offended by its portrayal of young love.

A number of collections of short essays and articles, many of which had previously been published, appeared in the years after the war. Colette was a master of the essay, demonstrating her extraordinary ability to create incisive and evocative portraits of friends and colleagues. There was a portrait of Proust, who at midnight at the Ritz seemed to be 'disturbed as if by a fierce wind', with his hat pushed back onto the nape of his neck, his shirt rumpled, his cravat flowing, and 'a fine black ash' deposited in the 'creases of his cheek, the sockets of his eyes and his panting mouth'.

Jean Cocteau, her close friend and neighbour, came under this penetrating gaze, which sought to reveal the character through its physical manifestation. There he was, 'with his crest of wavy hair, lean like a greyhound, his sleeve rolled up to reveal hands like vines'. Another neighbour, the actor Jean Marais, who was performing the role of Chéri in a new theatrical adaptation of her work, appeared in her room as 'a tall archangel' who had to 'fold his wings that bump into the doorframe and burn against the skylights'.

She described visits from Marguerite Moreno. Their friendship had cemented over many years as they had toured and performed together. Moreno was still performing in the theatre and on film, and had achieved great success, most notably in Giraudoux's *La Folle de Chaillot* (*The Madwoman of Chaillot*) in 1946. She would climb up my staircase, Colette wrote, and come inside, 'adorned in her usual way—cigarette, felt hat pulled

Marguerite Moreno in the late 1930s

Top, Colette and Maurice working; below, Colette at Le Grand Véfour in 1950, with Jean Marais and Valentine Tessier, celebrating the stage revival of Chéri

down over one eye, overcoat the colour of dusk and rain. Always true to herself, ready to set off again and again, overworked and full of endurance.'

Moreno's and Colette's correspondence is one of the most moving testaments to friendship. Their letters span forty-six years, from 1902 to Moreno's death in 1948. 'I search for her around me,' wrote Colette after her death. When she had been alive, they could go for long periods of time without seeing each other, but a telephone call or an exchange of letters made the space between them 'sonorous and limpid'. Now the 'powerful musical voice, the long vibration of Alexandrines, had fallen silent'.

Another friend and colleague was Léon-Paul Fargue. This poet, friend of the symbolists and of the composer Ravel, was a true Parisian. He published two books about the city—*D'après Paris* in 1931 and *Le Piéton de Paris* in 1939. Colette had met him in the 1920s and they remained friends throughout their lives. 'I never saw Léon-Paul Fargue except at night,' she wrote. He was like a nocturnal bird, coming to life after dark, 'his eyes completely filling vast deep sockets'.

Colette described going to visit Fargue one evening with Maurice, across the streets of Paris, the 'uncontested realm' of this poet, streets of powdery gold as the sun set. This poet of the streets of Paris was now confined to his lodging amongst the plane trees on rue Montparnasse, where he charmed Colette, Goudeket and his other guests over a convivial dinner, a meal which each of them knew would not be repeated. Fargue died in 1947.

Pour un herbier, first published in 1949 and again in 1951 in an edition illustrated by Raoul Dufy, was written on commission. A Swiss publisher proposed to send Colette flowers, once or twice a week over the period of a year or so. If she was moved to do so, she would write a portrait of one of the flowers and the publisher would put them together into a book. Colette was not able to resist such an invitation, and the work evolved in response to the flowers delivered from a nearby florist, orchids brought by her daughter, a long branch of wisteria from the old vine at Saint-Sauveur.

The charming little collection is thus made up of flowers, memories and botanical digressions. A tulip is like a painted Easter egg, marigolds (*souci* in French) remind her of her little dog called Souci, the streets of Paris celebrate the first day of May with people selling, for just a few cents, little bunches of lily of the valley to bring good luck. A potted white hyacinth reminds her of an expanse of blue hyacinths that looked like a flowering field of blue linen. The collection starts and ends with roses—the roses of the gardens of the Palais-Royal and the Christmas rose of the garden of her childhood.

One of the great delights of these later years of Colette's life was her friendship with Raymond Oliver, the owner-chef of the now fabled restaurant Le Grand Véfour. Colette had always been a lover of good food. Food connected her to place. In the South, garlic, oil and the three vegetables inseparable from Provençale cuisine—aubergine, tomatoes and red peppers—made for an ideal repast. In Brittany, she indulged in the *fruits de mer*, as the French call them, the fruits of the sea—oysters, lobsters, shrimp. Colette's *gourmandise* was part of her way of being in the present, savouring every moment, abolishing the passage of time and giving into the luxury of slowing down.

Raymond Oliver took over the former Café de Chartres on the ground floor of the Palais-Royal in 1948. From its grand days at the time of the Second Empire, it had fallen into a state of decline. Oliver and his wife restored the restaurant to its former glory, and quickly established a friendship with Colette and many other residents in the Palais-Royal. Colette's *gourmandise* met her equal in Raymond Oliver, who was both a traditionalist and an innovator in his approach to cooking. He was from Gascony in the south-west, and he and Colette enjoyed many discussions about recipes and food, comparing the different tastes and culinary accents of their native provinces, Gascony and Burgundy. From time to time, Oliver would cook something special for a handful of privileged friends—and he would always keep some aside for Colette. One day he sent up to her a 'stunning, homely *cassoulet*, gratinéed on top and mellow underneath, a *cassoulet* for neighbours and connoisseurs'. Thank you, she wrote, and 'may it be our good luck that you never leave!'

Colette and Raymond Oliver also enjoyed sharing a good bottle of Pommery. She loved to hear the pop of the champagne cork and to see 'rising up from the depths of the golden wine, bubbles like laughter', 'pearls of bouncing air'. Oliver would pop up the stairs to visit her, or two of his white-vested staff would carry her down the stairs and along the colonnade to the restaurant in a special portable chair. Oliver wrote that as soon as Colette arrived in Le Grand Véfour, her eyes dramatically made up, her mass of hair like whipped cream, with flashes of silver amongst the blue-grey, his worries would disappear. There was too much mischievous goodness in Colette to allow for any ill-humour.

Colette's seat in the corner table of this elegant restaurant is still named after her. Like Cocteau, Colette loved the sense of history and continuity embodied by Le Grand Véfour, with its Louis XVI ceiling, its mirrors and painted panels, its red velvet banquettes. At lunchtime, she wrote, the sun lights up the colours of these

Colette in 1953, photographed by Janine Niepce

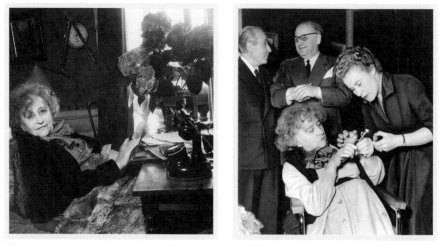

On her divan-bed   *With her daughter, on her eightieth birthday*

painted panels, which a century of gastronomy has not faded. There is a sense that you have entered into another time when you pass through the velvet curtained entrance to this beautiful room—a time when you can leave your troubles behind and just indulge your senses. Colette's mischievous good humour, her sense of occasion and her love of good food and good wine, still live on at Le Grand Véfour.

Food, friendship and a constant fascination with the world around her sustained Colette through these last years, when she was forced to spend so much time in her room. The walls were hung with red silk. Her divan-bed was next to the window so that she could look out onto the garden below. Her writing table, given to her twenty-five years earlier by the Princesse de Polignac, straddled her bed so that she could work there. On it sat her little blue pot with her collection of pens, her blue writing paper, books, perhaps her embroidery, her reading glasses. Hanging on the wall next to the bed was an old-fashioned barometer. On the mantelpiece opposite, reflected in the mirror behind them, was her collection of glass paperweights—with their intricate patterns and myriad colours. 'A paperweight has some of the qualities of pure art because of its uselessness,' she wrote. The bookshelf behind her held a globe and her favourite books—reference books about flowers, plants and animals, books recounting the incredible voyages of early travellers to distant lands—together with her framed butterflies. Throughout the apartment were paintings given to her by artist friends.

Colette thought that *L'Etoile vesper* (*The Evening Star*), published in 1946, would be her last book. At the end of it, she wrote about her obsession, her duty to write: 'the

obsession, the sense of obligation, I have lived with them for half a century … How difficult it is to put a stop to one's own being.'

She had taken up embroidery, thinking this would be a distraction from writing, but she recognised that pen and needle would continue to go hand in hand as she moved slowly towards the end of her road.

Le Fanal bleu (*The Blue Lantern*) appeared in 1949. She had planned to write a journal, but she soon realised that she didn't know how to go about it. Her writing was a process of reflection, memory and observation. It focused on the everyday— on the people who came to visit her, the treatments she was undergoing for her arthritis, the letters she received, a visit to friends in Beaujolais. It was the ordinary that interested Colette and aroused her curiosity. And yet, from the ordinary she fashioned something extraordinary through the power of her writing. And writing was what she would continue to do. 'There is no other destiny for me,' she wrote. She had once believed that writing was the same as any other task. Having put down one's pen, one cried with joy, 'Finished,' only to see grains of sand falling from one's hands, tracing out the words, 'To be continued …' But this was to be her last work.

Cocteau was a regular visitor in the last years of Colette's life, and he described her gradual decline in his own *Journal*. She was retreating into what he called her 'cloud', but from within this cloud she knew very well that she was in control. Her childlike helplessness was just a game, and she still had all her wits about her. Colette took advantage of being immobile, he wrote, of being a bit deaf, of not being aware of what was going on around her, of having Maurice as her filter to the wider world. But there were moments when her fine eyes would flash, like those of a sick lioness. It was Claudine on the alert. Much more alive, Cocteau wrote, than the lady of letters who has taken up embroidery. Cocteau was never duped by the grand old lady that Colette had become. For him, she had never stopped being the young woman who had danced semi-naked, who had scandalised Paris with her lesbian affairs, and who had resolutely defied convention to forge her own destiny.

Colette's eightieth birthday in January 1953 was celebrated with more honours. She was promoted to the rank of Grand Officer of the Legion of Honour, and she received the Grand Medal of the City of Paris. The American Ambassador to France presented her with the Diploma of the National Institute of Arts and Letters. The literary pages of the newspapers carried tributes written by many of her peers.

But slowly her flame of life was ebbing. Colette was becoming more distracted, less lucid. In February 1954, she and Maurice travelled to Monte Carlo, where they stayed for several months in the Hôtel de Paris. Holidaying in Monte Carlo at the Hôtel de Paris had been an annual tradition that Maurice and Colette had enjoyed since 1950, but this would be their last visit. She took pleasure in the gardens and in presenting, for the last time, the Monaco literary prize, of which she was the honorary president.

When they returned to Paris, Colette's life relentlessly drew to a close. She died on 3 August 1954. At her bedside were Maurice, Pauline and her daughter, Colette.

In spite of the representations of many people, including Graham Greene, who wrote an open letter to the Archbishop of Paris, Colette was refused a church funeral. She was accorded, however, the first state funeral ever granted to a woman by the French Republic, and ten thousand people paid homage to her as her body lay in state. Her funeral was held on Saturday 7 August, in the courtyard of the Palais-Royal, with speeches and the trumpeters of the National Guard playing Chopin's *Funeral March*. She was buried in Père Lachaise cemetery.

Towards the end of her life, Colette had written that she would love to start all over again. 'These last seventy-nine years haven't always been comfortable,' she wrote, 'but how quickly they have passed.' Colette was a gourmand for life—there was never enough of it for her—and she left behind a literary oeuvre that is brimming with life, and with the struggles and triumphs of living.

Hers was a passionate life, the life of a woman who chose freedom and yet who knew that she had left behind her many shadows—her own and those of the people and places she loved.

I leave behind me, at each place where my desires have wandered, thousands
of shadows that look like me, plucked from me, this one on the warm blue stone
of the dells of my childhood, this one in the moist hollow of a sunless valley,
and this other one, which follows the birds and sails, the wind and the waves.
You will retain the most tenacious; a naked sinuous shadow, moving to the rhythm
of pleasure like grass in a stream. But time will dissolve this one like the others,
and you will know nothing more of me, until the days when my path comes to
an end and a last little shadow will fly away.

Magnifique, Marguerite ! J'ai
vu hier soir _La Dame de pique_.
Tu es un enseignement frappant de ce
qu'en devrait faire. Quand je vois,
au théâtre — surtout au théâtre — les
acteurs exprimer la vieillesse et l'épou-
vante, je vomis. Ta défaillance de la
fin, la grâce de ta méchanceté, tout
est exemplaire. Et puis c'est enfin
un rôle, qui commence quelque
part et qui va quelque part. Pour-
quoi n'en fait-on pas une pièce, de
la Dame ? Elle existe ? Je m'en
moque. Elle n'existe pas puisque
tu ne la joues pas. Évidemment
tu "fais jeune" pour le rôle ; mais
ça vaut mieux qu'un hideux

Epilogue —

Closing the circle

Epilogue

I am sitting in the gardens of the Palais-Royal looking up at Colette's window. I have come to the end of my journey through Colette's France, coming full circle, back to where I used to sit as a student many years ago.

My journey has taken me back to the nearby Bibliothèque nationale, where I have consulted manuscripts and newspaper clippings, photographs and other records. The library has changed a great deal in the intervening years. The domed reading room where I used to work is closed for renovations; some of the material I wanted to consult, including the beautifully illustrated editions of Colette's work, is now located in the imposing new François Mitterrand Library. This vast complex houses more than ten million volumes and is an outstanding piece of modern architecture, with its four 'book-end' towers and its sunken garden bordered by a wide corridor, off which all the reading rooms are located. I found myself going to and fro between the two libraries, the old and the new.

Back at the old library, there were changes in the neighbourhood. Many of the beautiful old *galeries*, the glass-roofed shopping arcades, have been renovated. There are new shops and restaurants. The little cheap workers' restaurant, Le Grand Colbert, where I would occasionally have lunch with other students, has been completely renovated, along with the nearby Galerie Vivienne and Galerie Colbert. It's now one of Paris's most famous—and touristy—restaurants, having been the setting for a scene in a Jack Nicholson and Diane Keaton movie. As students, we had taken the beautiful mosaic floor, mirrors and decorated pilasters for granted. I have occasionally been tempted to go back there, but I am reluctant to dislodge my memories of those cheap and cheerful meals. Instead, I go back to the little cafes where I used to have a baguette and coffee, or a little omelette and salad. I feel a nostalgic joy to be back in the neighbourhood.

The Colette I have come to know through this journey of rediscovery is a much more complex person than the one I knew as a young PhD student. She is also a very different person from the one who has been described in many of her biographies. It is easy to be captured by Colette's self-projection.

There have been times when I have not particularly liked the Colette that has revealed herself to me over this journey. How could she not have visited her mother more regularly when Sido was old and sick? Can her treatment of Missy be excused? Her neglect of her daughter? And what of the literary settling of accounts with Willy, and, indeed, with her second husband? Her narcissism dominates.

And yet, these are all part of the same Colette who was a loyal and generous friend, a revered mentor to many young writers, an inspiration for many women as they sought their own paths towards freedom and independence.

One of these younger women was Simone de Beauvoir. They met when Colette was seventy-five years old. Beauvoir had always admired her writing, finding in it a telling description of the situation of women and of female sexuality. For Beauvoir, Colette was a great writer, but also a woman who fought for her rights and, through her writing, achieved financial independence. She admired her audacity in describing women's sensuality and the compassion she showed to her young heroines who retained their pride even in the face of deception. It was through Beauvoir that a whole generation of women were reintroduced to Colette as a feminist writer, even though Colette herself always denied having any interest in feminism.

More recently, the French critic Julia Kristeva devoted a volume of her trilogy on female genius to Colette. For Kristeva, Colette's genius lay in her art, in her transposition of sensual pleasure into words, into what she herself had called a new alphabet, an alphabet which unites everything in a poetry of the physical world, where love is transposed into art. Like the nightingale, which sings all through the night to keep itself awake so that it not become entwined within the tendrils of the vine, Colette wrote in order to free herself from the shackles of any form of dependence and to celebrate a very female enjoyment of all the pleasures that life can offer. Nothing lasts except through style, Colette wrote.

The Colette that I have come to know through this journey is a Colette who realised early in her life that she alone was responsible for her own happiness, and that she would not hesitate to take that happiness wherever and whenever it offered itself to her. As her mother wrote to her, her life was far from banal and it certainly wasn't easy. But from this tough, rich and varied life, she created works that are as generous and full of energy in their rendering of the pleasures and passion of life as she was in her love of the world around her.

Epilogue

Colette was greedy for life and she did not stand back from the opportunities it presented to her. Her tenacity, her perseverance, her single-minded pursuit of her own interests were what made her the great writer she was. To the end, she resisted any form of self-pity, even when she was in great pain. Her pain was just another thing worthy of her fierce attention, of being translated, like so much else, into words.

Through her work, Colette revealed her admiration for everything that fights hard to hold on to life. She looked at the world with detachment, seeing things for what they were and not shirking from describing them as she saw them. She was never beholden to anyone else's ideas of what was right or wrong, and she had an innate sense of restraint and moral certainty. Not for her 'the narrow domain of obscenity, where one so quickly becomes stifled and bored', as she wrote in 1932 about the recent translation into French of *Lady Chatterley's Lover*. Two years before her death, she said in an interview: 'Perhaps the most praiseworthy thing about me is that I have known how to write like a woman, without anything moralistic or theoretical, without promulgating.'

Colette loved the infiniteness of a world that was always at her fingertips—the miracle of an opening flower, the musty smell of water chestnuts, the sigh of a dropping petal. Her work celebrated the natural world, the pleasures of the senses. It also plumbed the depths of human feelings, the unspoken secrets of human relationships. Her depictions of human emotions—jealousy, greed, disappointment, love in all its forms, and most especially courage in the face of adversity—were enriched by her own life experiences. She was recognised for her stylistic brilliance, and yet she wrote often of the difficulty of writing.

As I have been researching the photos for this book, I have been reminded constantly of Colette's incredibly strong sense of self. Her photos project a powerful magnetism, the sense of a woman who knew her power to seduce, whether through words or looks. Julien Green, who visited her in 1951, described her eyes as the most beautiful of any woman he knew, brimming with soul and sadness. The photographer Gisèlle Freund wrote that Colette didn't care about being beautiful in her photos—what she wanted was to be fascinating. Angela Carter wrote of her 'alluring magnetism'. Colette had been a seductively beautiful young woman and she remained a seductively beautiful older woman, whose composed gaze never wavered.

Have I finished with Colette? I think not. I will always return with pleasure to the vigour and lucidity of her prose. I will always be curious to learn more of what lies behind the many masks of this complex and fascinating woman, and to delve deeper into the wisdom of her imaginary world.

My journey through Colette's France has been coloured and perfumed by Colette's nostalgia for, and re-creation of, the past, together with her indomitable spirit and zest for life. Death didn't interest her, particularly not her own. I am alive, she wrote, and so I have a duty to be happy.

Everything that astonished me when I was young astonishes me even more today. The time will never come for me when there are no more discoveries to make. Every morning the world is as new again and I will not cease to flower except through death.

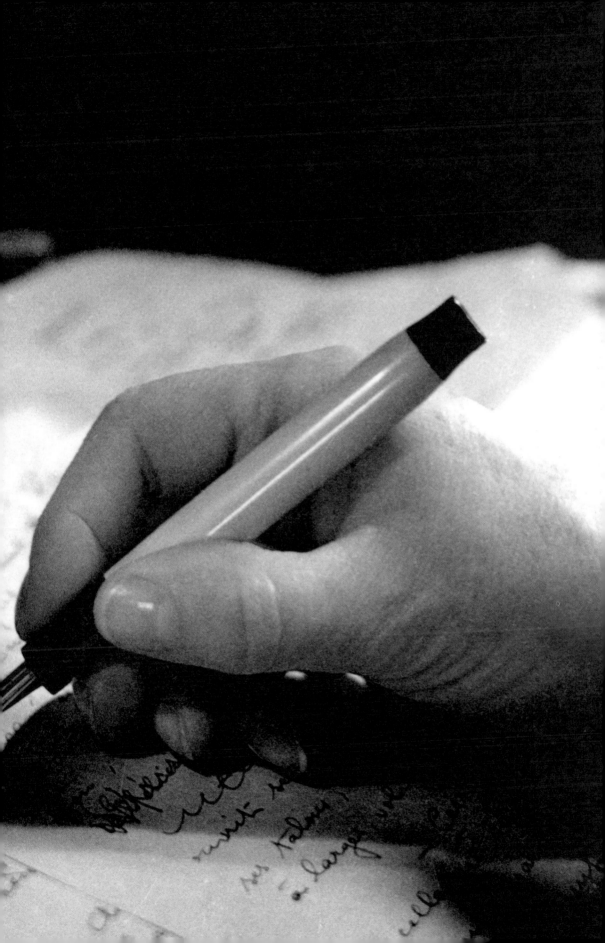

Chronology

1829	Birth of Jules-Joseph Colette, Colette's father, in Toulon
1835	Birth of Adèle-Eugénie-Sidonie 'Sido' Landoy, Colette's mother, in Paris
1857	Marriage of Sidonie Landoy and Jules Robineau-Duclos, property owner in the Puisaye
1860	Birth of Juliette Robineau-Duclos, Colette's half-sister
1863	Birth of Achille Robineau-Duclos, Colette's half-brother
1865	Death of Jules Robineau-Duclos
	Marriage of Sidonie Landoy and Captain Jules-Joseph Colette
1868	Birth of Léopold 'Léo' Colette, Colette's brother
1873	Birth of Sidonie-Gabrielle Colette on 28 January in the family home on rue de l'Hospice (now rue Colette) in Saint-Sauveur
1891	The family leaves Saint-Sauveur for Châtillon-Coligny
1893	Marriage of Sidonie-Gabrielle Colette and Henry 'Willy' Gauthier-Villars
	Colette moves to Paris, where she and Willy set up house in an apartment at 28 rue Jacob
1895	Colette and Willy are invited to Saint-Sauveur for the prize-giving ceremony at the school
1900	*Claudine à l'école*, the first of the *Claudine* books, is published under Willy's name
1901	The couple moves to 93, and then 177 bis, rue de Courcelles
1902	Willy purchases Le Domaine des Monts-Bouccons, near Besançon
1903	*Claudine s'en va*, the last of the *Claudine* books, is published under Willy's name
1904	*Dialogue de bêtes* is published, with Colette signing the book Colette Willy
1905	Death of Colette's father
1906	Separation of Colette and Willy
	Colette moves to 44 rue Villejust
	Colette's first appearance at the Théâtre des Mathurins in *Le Désir, l'Amour et la Chimère*
1910	Missy purchases Rozven in Brittany
	Divorce proclaimed between Colette and Henry Gauthier-Villars
	Publication of *La Vagabonde*
	Colette begins writing for *Le Matin*, where she meets Henry de Jouvenel

1911	Rupture with Missy
1912	Death of Colette's mother, Sido
	Marriage with Henry de Jouvenel
1913	Birth of Colette de Jouvenel, daughter of Colette and Henry de Jouvenel
1914	Henry de Jouvenel is mobilised with the army
1920	*Chéri* is published
	Colette receives the award of Chevalier of the Legion of Honour
1923	*Le Blé en herbe* (*The Ripening Seed*) is published, signed simply Colette for the first time
	Colette returns to the theatre, performing in adaptations of her own work, *Chéri* and later *La Vagabonde*
	Separation between Colette and Henry de Jouvenel
1925	First performance of *L'Enfant et les sortilèges* (*The Child and the Magic Spells*), libretto by Colette and music by Maurice Ravel, in Monte Carlo
	Colette and Maurice Goudeket holiday together in the South of France
1926	Colette buys La Treille Muscate, near Saint-Tropez, and sells Rozven
1927	Colette moves into the mezzanine apartment at 9 rue de Beaujolais (Palais-Royal)
1928	*La Naissance du jour* is published
1930	*Sido* is published
1931	Colette moves to Claridge's on the Champs-Élysées
	Death of Willy
1932	Colette opens her beauty salon at 6 rue de Miromesnil in Paris
	Publication of *Ces plaisirs*, later republished as *Le Pur et l'impur*
1933	Colette begins writing fortnightly theatre reviews for *Le Journal*; these are later published in four volumes as *La Jumelle noire* (*The Black Opera Glasses*) from 1934 to 1938
1935	Colette and Maurice Goudeket marry
	Death of Henry de Jouvenel
1936	Colette is promoted to rank of Commander of the Legion of Honour
	Colette is elected to the Belgian Royal Academy of French Language and Literature, replacing the poet Anna de Noailles
1938	Colette moves to the first-floor apartment in the Palais-Royal, 9 rue de Beaujolais
	Sale of La Treille Muscate

1940   Colette and Goudeket leave Paris for Bel-Gazou's castle at Curemonte after the occupation of Paris by the Germans; they return three months later in September

1941   Goudeket is arrested by the Germans

1942   Goudeket is released from Compiègne and returns to Paris

1945   Colette is elected unanimously as a member of the Académie Goncourt

1948   Death of Colette's close friend, Marguerite Moreno

1953   Colette turns eighty, and receives the Grand Medal of the City of Paris and the award of Grand Officer of the Legion of Honour

1954   Death of Colette on 3 August

Colette's state funeral is held on 7 August, and she is buried in Père Lachaise cemetery

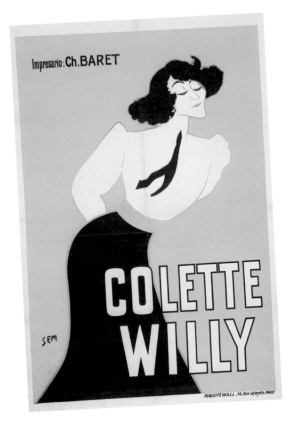

WORKS BY COLETTE

There have been three editions of Colette's collected works in French:

Oeuvres complètes, 15 vols, Paris, Le Fleuron, 1948–50

Oeuvres, 3 vols, Paris, Flammarion, 1960

Oeuvres, 4 vols, Paris, Bibliothèque de la Pléiade, 1984–2001

The following is a selection of individual works by Colette available in English. As can be seen from their publication dates, a number of these have recently been reissued.

The Complete Claudine: Claudine at School, Claudine in Paris, Claudine Married, Claudine and Annie, translated by Antonia White, New York, Farrar, Straus and Giroux, 2001

The Vagabond, translated by Stanley Applebaum, New York, Farrar, Straus and Giroux, 2010

Chéri and *The Last of Chéri*, translated by Roger Senhouse, New York, Farrar, Straus and Giroux, 2001

The Pure and the Impure, translated by Herma Briffault, New York, New York Review of Books Classics, 2000

Break of Day, translated by Enid McLeod, New York, Farrar, Straus and Giroux, 2002

My Mother's House and Sido, translated by Enid McLeod and Una Vicenza Troubridge, New York, Farrar, Straus and Giroux, 2002

The Ripening Seed, translated by Roger Senhouse, London, Penguin Classics, 1995

The Blue Lantern, translated by Roger Senhouse, New York, Farrar, Straus and Giroux, 1963

The Evening Star: Recollections, translated by David Le Vay, New York, Colliers, 1986

Gigi and *The Cat*, translated by Roger Senhouse, Antonia White, London, Penguin Classics, 1995

The Collected Stories of Colette, edited by Robert Phelps, translated by Antonia White, Matthew Ward, Anne-Marie Callimachi, New York, Farrar, Straus and Giroux, 1984

LETTERS

There have been a number of collections of Colette's letters published in French. Of these, I have drawn particularly on the following:

Lettres à Hélène Picard, edited by Claude Pichois, Paris, Flammarion, 1958

Lettres à Marguerite Moreno, edited by Claude Pichois, Paris, Flammarion, 1959

Lettres de la vagabonde, edited by Claude Pichois and Roberte Forbin, Paris, Flammarion, 1961 (Letters to Léon Hamel, Georges Wague and Léopold Marchand and his wife, Misz)

Lettres au petit corsaire, edited by Claude Pichois and Roberte Forbin, Paris, Flammarion, 1963 (Letters to Renée Hamon)

Lettres à ses pairs, edited by Claude Pichois and Roberte Forbin, Paris, Flammarion, 1973 (Letters between Colette and her friends who were writers, artists or musicians)

Lettres à Annie de Pène et Germaine Beaumont, edited by Francine Dugast, Paris, Flammarion, 1995

Lettres à sa fille, edited by Anne de Jouvenel, Paris, Gallimard, 2003 (Letters between Colette and her daughter)

Lettres à Missy, edited by Samia Bordji and Frédéric Maget, Paris, Flammarion, 2009

Sido: Lettres à Colette, edited by Gérard Bonal, Paris, Libella, 2012 (Letters from Sido)

BOOKS ABOUT COLETTE

The following is a personal selection of the many books written about Colette in French and English over the years.

Bonal, Gérard, and Maget, Frédéric, editors. *Colette*, Paris, Editions de l'Herne, 2011

Bonal, Gérard, and Remy-Bieth, Michel. *Colette Intime*, Paris, Editions Phébus, 2004

Castillo, Michel del. *Colette, une certaine France*, Paris, Editions Stock, 1999

Clement, Marie-Christine, and Didier. *Colette Gourmande*, Paris, Albin Michel, 1990

Crosland, Margaret. *Colette, The Difficulty of Loving*, New York, Bobbs-Merrill, 1973

Goudeket, Maurice. *Près de Colette*, Paris, Flammarion, 1956

Kristeva, Julia. *Colette*, translated by Jane Marie Todd, New York, Columbia University Press, 2004

Pichois, Claude, and Brunet, Alain. *Colette*, Paris, Editions de Fallois, 1999

Thurman, Judith. *Secrets of the Flesh, A Life of Colette*, New York, Alfred A. Knopf, 1999

OTHER SOURCES AND REFERENCES

Barney, Natalie Clifford. *Souvenirs indiscrets*, Paris, Flammarion, 1960

Beauvoir, Simone de. 'Lettre à Nelson Algren', in *Colette*, edited by Gérard Bonal and Frédéric Maget, Paris, Editions de l'Herne, 2011

Beauvoir, Simone de. *The Second Sex*, translated by Constance Borde and Sheila Malovaney-Chevalier, New York, Alfred A. Knopf, 2010

Cocteau, Jean. *My contemporaries*, translated by Margaret Crosland, Peter Owen Publishers, London, 2008

Cocteau, Jean. *Le Passé défini, Journal*, 3 vols, edited by Pierre Chanel, Paris, Gallimard, 1953

Oliver, Raymond. *Adieu fourneaux*, Paris, R. Laffont, 1984

Weiss, Andrea. *Paris was a Woman*, London, Harper Collins, 1995

IN PARIS

Colette had many addresses in Paris, and some of the buildings no longer exist. Plaques record her period as resident at the two following addresses:

28 rue Jacob

She lived here for three years (1893 to 1896) following her arrival in Paris as the wife of Willy.

9 rue de Beaujolais, Palais-Royal

She lived firstly on the mezzanine floor (1926 to 1930) and then on the first floor (1938 to 1954).

palais-royal.monuments-nationaux.fr

Restaurant Drouant

The Académie Goncourt still meets for their monthly meetings at this restaurant. place Gaillon, 75002

www.drouant.com

Le Grand Véfour

From the time Raymond Oliver took over the restaurant in 1948 until her death, Colette was a frequent visitor, even when she had to be carried downstairs in a specially designed chair. Now run by chef Guy Martin, it is one of Paris's best and most beautiful restaurants.

17, rue de Beaujolais, Palais-Royal

www.grand-vefour.com

Père Lachaise Cemetery

Colette is buried here, with her daughter.

www.pere-lachaise.com

IN SAINT-SAUVEUR-EN-PUISAYE

Saint-Sauveur is a bit over two hours' drive from Paris, or you can take the train to Auxerre and hire a car to complete the thirty-minute drive to the village. There are no hotels in Saint-Sauveur, but there are a couple of charming bed and breakfasts in the village and neighbourhood.

Musée Colette

The museum is closed from 1 November to 31 March; check the website for opening hours.

Château, 89520, Saint-Sauveur-en-Puisaye

www.musee-colette.com

Société des Amis de Colette

This site will have information about the house where Colette was born, which is expected to open in late 2013.

www.amisdecolette.fr

Centre d'Etudes Colette

www.centre-colette.fr

IN BESANÇON

Le Domaine des Monts-Bouccons

Not open to the public.

Besançon is a very attractive town with its well-preserved old centre, the citadel and its many museums. It is two-and-a-halfhours by train from Paris.

IN BRITTANY

Rozven

Close to Saint-Coulomb, on the coast road between Cancale and Saint-Malo. From Cancale, take the D201 towards Saint-Malo. Just past the turn-off on the left to Saint-Coulomb (the D74), there is a little track to the right. Park your car and walk down the track to the beach, from where you can see Rozven.

In Cancale, we stayed at **La Maison de la Marine**, a charming small hotel situated in the old customs house building at the top of the town. The dining room has a magnificent seafaring-inspired décor and the gastronomy is highly regarded.

www.maisondelamarine.com/en

IN THE CORRÈZE
Château de Castel-Novel
Now a four-star hotel in the Relais et Châteaux group, a 15-minute drive from Brive-la-Gaillarde. It is run by Sophie Parveaux-Soulié, with her husband Nicolas Soulié as chef.
www.castelnovel.com

Les Jardins de Colette
The gardens are just a couple of minutes by car from Castel-Novel (or within walking distance). They are open from 1 April to 30 October. Check the website for opening times, which change depending on the month.
www.lesjardinsdecolette.com

IN SAINT-TROPEZ
La Treille Muscate
Not open to the public. All you can see is the gate with the name of the house. It is on the Route des Salins, on the corner formed by the Chemin de l'Estagnet.

There are many places to stay in and around Saint-Tropez. The Hotel de la Ponche is a four-star hotel in the old town, an ideal location to get a feeling for Saint-Tropez as it once was. www.laponche.com

Rondini
This is where Colette bought her sandals, which she wore all year round.
16 rue Georges Clemenceau

Musée de l'Annonciade
Has a small but excellent collection of the works of painters, many of whom who lived and worked around Saint-Tropez in the period 1890 to 1950.

In the hinterland around Saint-Tropez are many charming little villages which Colette loved to visit—Ramatuelle, Gassin, Grimaud.

CHAMBRE D'HÔTEL

BELLA - VISTA

MES APPRENTISSAGES

LA JUMELLE NOIRE

BELLES SAISONS

LE TOUTOUNIER

DUO

LA CHATTE

LE PUR ET L'IMPUR

NUDITÉ

PRISONS ET PARADIS

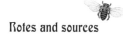

Notes and sources

Translations from Colette's work and correspondence are by the author.

The illustrations reproduced are from the three-volume *Oeuvres de Colette,* published by Flammarion in 1960. Some of these pictures had previously appeared in illustrated editions published during Colette's lifetime.

The photographs are drawn from various private and public collections. Particular mention is made of the generous permission granted by the Centre d'Étude Colette, M. Michel Remy-Bieth and M. Foulques de Jouvenel for the use of material from their collections.

Quotations

p 12   *La Vagabonde*
p 30   *La Maison de Claudine*
p 32   *La Maison de Claudine*
p 35   Letter to Marguerite Moreno, April 1923, *Lettres à Marguerite Moreno*
p 38   *Paysages et portraits*
p 44   *Trois … six … neuf*
p 68   *Mes apprentissages*
p 75   Article published in *Les Tablette*s, 1911
p 80   *Mes apprentissages*
p 84   *La Vagabonde*
p 95   André Parinaud: sound recording 2004, Bibliothèque nationale de France
p 97   *Bella-Vista*
p 104   Letter to Léopold Marchand, 28 April 1921, *Lettres de la Vagabonde*
p 104   Renaud de Jouvenel, article published in *La Revue de Paris,* December, 1966
p 106   Letters to Renaud de Jouvenel, *La Revue de Paris,* 1966
p 126   *La Vagabonde*
p 132   *La Naissance du jour*
p 136   *Le Pur et l'impur*
p 142   Letter to Madame Léopold Marchand, 15 July 1938, *Lettres de la Vagabonde*
p 140   *En pays connu*
p 151   *L'Étoile Vesper*
p 152   Francis Carco, preface to *Paris de ma fenêtre*
p 156   *Le Fanal bleu*
p 166   *La Vagabonde*
p 175   Speech for the opening night of the film of *Le Blé en herbe,* directed by
        Claude Autant-Lara in 1954

PHOTOGRAPHIC AND ILLUSTRATION CREDITS

p ii   © Henri Manuel/Roger-Viollet/Foulques de Jouvenel

p iv   From top, photographs by the author; covers of the Claudine novels, Centre d'Étude Colette

p v   Photograph by the author

p viii   Postcard of Saint-Tropez and poster, Centre d'Étude Colette

p 1   Centre d'Étude Colette

p 3   Portrait by Henri Carrere, © Rue des Archives/CCI

p 6   © Laure Albin Guillot/Roger-Viollet

p 10   Postcard of Saint-Sauveur, Centre d'Étude Colette

p 11   Colette at the age of five, Centre d'Étude Colette

p 13   top, bottom left and right, Centre d'Étude Colette

p 15   Centre d'Étude Colette

p 16–17 View of Saint-Sauveur, Collection Gamma-Rapho, © Getty Images

p 18   Colette at eighteen months, annotated by Colette: 'how charming I was when I was 18 months old'. Centre d'Étude Colette

p 20   Centre d'Étude Colette

p 21   Centre d'Étude Colette

p 24   Collection of Michel Remy-Bieth

p 25   Collection of Michel Remy-Bieth

p 27   Centre d'Étude Colette

p 31   © Grau Sala, *Oeuvres de Colette*, vol. 3, Flammarion

p 32   Willy visiting the Colette family in Châtillon, Collection of Michel Remy-Bieth

p 33   Colette at the age of eighteen, Collection of Michel Remy-Bieth

p 35   Centre d'Étude Colette

p 38   Centre d'Étude Colette

p 41   Colette, her parents and brothers on the front steps in Châtillon, Centre d'Étude Colette

p 42–3   The woods that 'roll on like waves', photograph by the author

p 44   Cover for *Claudine s'en va*, illustration by Eugene Pascau, Collection of Michel Remy-Bieth

p 45   Collection of Michel Remy-Bieth

p 47   Parc Monceau, photographs by the author

p 48   © Andre Dignimont/ADAGP. Licensed by Viscopy, 2013

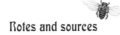

p 51   Colette at around the time of her marriage to Willy, © Rue des Archives/
        Tallandier

p 52   Plaque at 28 rue Jacob, where Colette lived in the early years of her literary
        life in Paris. It reads: 'Dark, seductive in the way of places that have stifled
        too many souls…' (*Mes apprentissages*). Photograph by the author

p 53   Café de Flore, photograph by the author

p 54   Centre d'Étude Colette

p 56–7 Parc Monceau, photograph by the author

p 58   Centre d'Étude Colette

p 59   Collection of Michel Remy-Bieth

p 61   © Rue des Archives/PVDE

p 62   From left, Centre d'Étude Colette; Collection of Michel Remy-Bieth,
        Centre d'Étude Colette

p 65   Musée Art Nouveau, Maxim's, photographs by the author

p 67   Illustration for the cover of *Claudine à l'école* by Emilio della Sudda,
        collection of Michel Remy-Bieth

p 68   Handwritten note from Colette to the pharmacist in Besançon.
        Colette loved to use decorative notepaper. Bibliothèque de Besançon,
        with thanks to Mme Marie-Claire Vaille

p 69   Colette in about 1910, © Musée Richard Anacréon, Granville

p 71   Sketch courtesy of the City of Besançon, photographs by the author

p 72–3 Photograph by Gabriel Vieille, City of Besançon

p 74   Centre d'Étude Colette

p 75   Photograph, Bibliothèque nationale de France

p 79   Colette in the gymnasium she had installed at rue de Courcelles,
        © Rue des Archives/RDA

p 81   Centre d'Étude Colette

p 83   © Andre Dignimont/ADAGP. Licensed by Viscopy, 2013

p 84   Photograph by the author; Poster for *Claudine*, collection of Michel Remy-
        Bieth

p 85   As the faun in *Le Désir, l'Amour et le Chimère*, © Lipnitzki/Roger-Viollet

p 87   Photographs by the author

p 88   Photograph of Missy and poster, collection of Michel Remy-Bieth

p 89   From top, Collection Jouvenel, Centre d'Étude Colette; collection of
        Michel Remy-Bieth

p 148   © Pierre Jahan/Getty Images

p 152–3 © Manuel Frères/Getty Images

p 154   top, Centre d'Étude Colette; bottom left and right, Collection of Michel Remy-Bieth

p 155   Centre d'Étude Colette

p 156   © Serge Lido/SIPA

p 159   Collection of Michel Remy-Bieth

p 160   Photographs by Matt Collins and the author; postcard, Centre d'Étude Colette

p 161   Colette in 1948, © Rue Des Archives/AGIP

p 163   © René Saint Paul/Rue des Archives

p 164   top, © Serge Lido/SIPA; bottom, Centre d'Étude Colette

p 165   Collection of Michel Remy-Bieth

p 166   top and bottom, Centre d'Étude Colette

p 168   © Janine Niepce/Roger-Viollet

p 170   left and right, Centre d'Étude Colette

p 173   © Gamma-Rapho via Getty Images

p 174–5 Photograph by the author

p 176   Letter to Marguerite Moreno, Centre d'Étude Colette

p 177   Colette in the 1930s, Collection of Michel Remy-Bieth

p 178   Photograph by the author

p 180   Photograph by the author

p 183   © Serge Lido/SIPA

p 184–5 © Walter Limot/Rue des Archives

p 186   Photograph by the author

p 189   Poster for theatre tour, collection of Michel Remy-Bieth

p 190   Centre d'Étude Colette

p 191   1903–04, dressed as a dandy with Toby-Chien, Collection of Michel Remy-Bieth

p 192–3 Photographs by the author

p 194   Photograph by the author

p 197   Photograph by the author

p 198   Photograph by the author

p 206   Photograph by the author

Acknowledgements

Many people have provided assistance, advice and encouragement as I have worked on this book. I am particularly indebted to Mme Samia Bordji, the Director of the Centre d'Etude Colette, who welcomed me so warmly on my first return visit to Saint-Sauveur-en-Puisaye, and has been generous in her continuing advice, and particularly in granting permission to reprint photographs and documents from the Centre's collection. Very special thanks also to M. Michel Remy-Bieth for very generously allowing me to reprint material from his extensive collection. He has been a collector of material relating to Colette since the 1950s, and his collection has shed light on many aspects of Colette's life that were, until recently, little known.

M. Foulques de Jouvenel encouraged me in this project and provided very helpful advice, putting me in touch with the current owners of Rozven and La Treille muscate. M. Frédéric Maget, the current President of the Society of Friends of Colette, was a warm and friendly correspondent. Madame Marie-Christine Clément and Didier Clément, the authors of *Colette Gourmand*, were gracious hosts when we visited their Grand Hôtel du Lion d'Or in Romorantin-Lanthenay. M. Lionel Estavoyer was a generous and informative guide in Besançon, and my thanks also go to Mme Christine Lauth, who welcomed us to La Treille muscate.

Various people have read the manuscript as the work has evolved. Special thanks to Iola Mathews, who has been a pillar of strength and practical advice, as well as to David Yencken and Jan McGuiness. Thanks also to Martine Hommey, whose apartment in Paris was our base when I was doing research there and who was inspired by my work to re-read Colette.

This book may not have eventuated but for a chance encounter with Sandy Grant of Hardie Grant. I thank him and Fran Berry, and most especially Helen Withycombe, for shepherding this book through from a good idea to the finished product. It has been a pleasure to work with everyone at Hardie Grant. Janet Austin was a sensitive and attentive editor, and Clare O'Loughlin was responsible for the design concept that seems to have captured a certain essence of Colette.

Acknowledgements

Friends and family have never flagged in their support and encouragement. They are too numerous to mention by name. My final debt of gratitude goes to Terry Brain, who has been a constant support and companion throughout the process. Our travels through France in search of Colette have been a shared joy. I dedicate this book to him, to the memory of Jim Thynne, my former husband with whom I shared those early years in Paris, and to my mother, whose love and support throughout my life have always been a source of great strength.

Jane Gilmour, at Rozven

About the author

Dr Jane Gilmour has a personal passion and extensive knowledge of Colette and her life. Jane lived and studied in France for many years and completed her thesis on the writer there. When she returned to Australia, her career took her in different directions, and she had senior management and consulting roles in the arts and sustainability. In recent years, she has been in a position to revisit her interest in Colette, returning to France on a number of occasions to research and write this book and to visit the regions where Colette lived, loved and worked.